THE CITIZEN
AND
THE STATE

GEORGE J.
STIGLER

THE CITIZEN   Essays
AND   on
THE STATE   Regulation

The University
of Chicago Press
CHICAGO AND LONDON

GEORGE J. STIGLER is the Charles
R. Walgreen Distinguished Service
Professor in the Department of
Economics and the Graduate School
of Business, The University of
Chicago. He was president of the
American Economic Association in
1964. He is the author of *The Theory
of Price, Capital and Rates of Return
in Manufacturing Industries,* and
Essays in the History of Economics
(University of Chicago Press, 1965).

The University of Chicago Press, Chicago 60637
The University of Chicago Press, Ltd., London

Library of Congress Cataloging in Publication Data

Stigler, George Joseph, 1911–
    The citizen and the State.

    Includes bibliographical references and index.
    1. Economic policy—Addresses, essays lectures.
I.   Title.
HD82.S834   338.9   74–33516
ISBN 0–226–77428–7

To
Aaron Director

Contents

Introduction

There cannot be many things in man's political history more ancient than the endeavor of governments to direct economic affairs. The need for state action—or the need for state withdrawal from action—has been a constant and fundamental theme of economics in its much shorter history. The endeavors of eighteenth-century England to direct economic policy called forth the splendid scorn of Adam Smith as he wrote the first and greatest masterpiece in economics. His successors continued to cultivate the policy area, and it has been a rare economist of importance whose opinions on economic policy were not well known to his contemporaries.

A persuasive case can be made that our strong interest in economic policy has not been reciprocated by a corresponding interest in economists' views by our society. One may suggest the support for this view by citing the widespread disregard of what is still the widely held preference of economists for free international trade. The customary reasons for the political disregard of professional economic opinion have been that (1) our theories are incomprehensible, and (2) "special interests" triumph in the political process. The former explanation is most unconvincing; our theories are not *that* difficult, and more difficult theories of physical scientists are accepted with alacrity. The second is a question rather than an answer: which interests control public policy, and why? Doubts such as these gradually grew upon me and created dissatisfaction with the traditional role which we economists have played in the discussion of public policy. These essays reflect the development of my own thoughts on public regulation during the past fifteen years.

Let us consider for a moment the traditional role of the economist in public policy, in which he analyzes, with the aid of economic theory, a specific problem in policy. If he found that a competitive market did not solve the problem efficiently, he recommended that the state take over the solution of the problem —with never a serious question on the comparative efficiencies of market and government (see chapters 4 and 7). If the competitive market solved the problem well (a quite routine example, *not* reprinted here, is my article, "The Economics of Minimum Wage Legislation," the *American Economic Review*, 1946), the economist suitably lamented the intervention of the state. The idea that minimum wage laws were the expression not of confused benevolence but of the well-informed desires of particular regions and classes of workers was not seriously considered by economists.

Several studies in this volume were stimulated by a desire to pass beyond the formal economic theory to determine more precisely the effects of the policies actually adopted. In the first of these (chap. 5), Claire Friedland and I searched for the effects of regulation of electrical utility rates by state public service commissions, and in the second (chap. 6) the review of new issues by the Securities and Exchange Commission was studied to determine whether purchasers of these new issues were benefited by the SEC reviews. The study of the *announced* goals of a regulatory policy is useful work, and I am delighted that these essays contributed to the development of the now widespread practice of studying the actual effects of public policies.

Often, but of course by no means always, the public policies seem not to achieve much toward fulfilling their announced goals. We found little effect of public regulation on the level of electrical rates or rates of return on investments in utility stocks, or, in the second study, little benefit to the purchasers of new stock issues from the SEC reviews. Eventually the question insists upon posing itself: in such cases, why is the policy adopted and persisted in?

It seems unfruitful, I am now persuaded, to conclude from the studies of the effects of various policies that those policies which did not achieve their announced goals, or had perverse effects (as with a minimum wage law), are simply mistakes of the society. A policy adopted and followed for a long time, or followed by many different states, could not usefully be described as a mistake: eventually its real effects would become known to interested groups. To say that such policies are mistaken is to say that one cannot explain them. I now think, for example, that large industrial and commercial users of electricity were the chief beneficiaries of the state regulation of electrical rates (and in our essay there is some unintentional evidence supporting this hypothesis).

This line of thought leads directly to the view that there is a market for regulatory legislation—a political market, to be sure. Some groups (industries, occupations) stand to gain more than others from boons the state can confer, such as subsidies, control of entry of new firms, and price control—just as some industries gain more than other industries from forming a cartel. Again, some groups are better able than others to mobilize political power, whether through votes or money. Where high benefits join low costs, there we should expect early and strong public regulation. This is the explicit theme of chapter 8—and the implicit theme of chapter 11.

This new focus of economic studies of regulation changes the economists' role from that of reformer to that of student of political economy. The change seems to me eminently desirable. Until we understand *why* our society adopts its policies, we will be poorly equipped to give useful advice on how to change those policies. Indeed, some changes (such as free trade) presumably are unattainable without a fundamental restructuring of the political system which we are unable to describe. A measure of restraint in our advice on policy would seem to be dictated by a sense of responsibility on the economists' part, and not only by the sense of caution of the body politic to whom we address the advice.

Of course we shall not, and need not, abandon all policy advising until we have unraveled all of the mysteries of the political-regulatory process. The very measurement of the costs and benefits of a policy will influence opinion and policy: one perfectly tenable hypothesis is that a society supports its economists simply because they provide complex kinds of information with speed, elegance, and increasingly more tolerable accuracy. I go beyond this humble but useful role in prescribing how to enforce laws (chap. 10). In any event, the basic assumption of the present approach is not that the traditional theory of economics is unhelpful in studying regulation but, on the contrary, is most helpful when it is applied directly to the understanding of the regulatory process.

I wish to acknowledge two heavy debts. The first is to the remarkable group of colleagues at the University of Chicago who constitute a unique intellectual environment: in addition to that profoundly wise man to whom this book is dedicated, I must name Gary Becker, Ronald Coase, Harold Demsetz (now of UCLA), Milton Friedman, Reuben Kessel, William Landes, Peter Pashigian, Sam Peltzman, Richard Posner, and Lester Telser. My second debt is to Claire Friedland. She is listed as co-author of one paper (chap. 5), but in fact she is the full and indispensable co-author of every one of the empirical studies (chaps. 6, 8, and 9), and only her different economic philosophy keeps me from blaming her for much of the remainder of the essays.

George J. Stigler

ONE

The Debate Over Freedom

1   The Unjoined Debate

The controversy between conservatives and liberals in the United States is so ineffective that it is not serving the purposes of controversy. The quality of controversy is not only low but in fact declining, and what was once a meaningful debate is becoming completely unjoined. An unjoined debate is only an affront to the social intelligence. I intend to blame both parties for this failure, and I seek to contribute to their confrontation on several basic issues. Since I am undoubtedly conservative, and only hopefully fair-minded, you should be warned against that perennial and not always intentional gambit, the restatement of an issue in such a way that it has only one defensible side.

The use of the word *extremist* to characterize a man and his position on public affairs has become fashionable. A word such as this is used less to describe a position than to dispose of it.

An extreme view is one which is sufficiently different from the accepted view of the majority, or the range of views that encompasses the majority, so that few people hold views still more different. The purpose in labeling an individual an extremist is to put his views outside the range of discussion—they are simply too absurd to merit the attention of normal people. An extremist is an intellectual lunatic—allowed loose if he does not communicate violence, but without an admission ticket to ordinary discourse.

There is merit in excluding the lunatic from discourse. If a man tells me he is Napoleon, or for that matter Josephine, discussion would serve no purpose. If a man asserts that the Supreme Court is filled with loyal but well-disguised communists, I do not wish to spend time on him. Occasionally the lone dissenter with the absurd view will prove to be right—a Galileo with a better scheme of the universe, a Babbage with a workable computer—but if we gave each lunatic a full, meticulous hearing, we should be wasting vast time and effort. So long as we do not suppress the peaceful

Reprinted from the University of Chicago, *Chicago Today* (Winter 1966).

lunatic, we leave open the possibility that he may convince others that he is right.

If there is one lunatic in a village, there will be a hundred in a city and thousands in a nation. But they will not share the same views: each will be eccentric in his own way. A group of men will share a common outlook only because they share common factual beliefs and accept the same causal relationships. They must have tolerably reasonable logical processes in order to arrive at a common position. The larger the group, the more certain we can be that it is not *insane* in the sense of being divorced from apparent fact and plausible reasoning.

If a minority group rejects demonstrable truth—as when I do not allow my small child to be vaccinated—the majority may resort to coercion, or otherwise abandon rational discourse. But this is an ultimate sanction, and it is defensible only if two conditions are met: the majority must be absolutely convinced of the correctness of its view; and the mistaken minority must be very small. A decent majority must have a strong sense of self-discipline, and practice a self-denial of power except under the most urgent and unambiguous conditions.

This does not mean that large groups may not be mistaken in their facts or fallacious in their reasoning. Even majorities can be sadly wrong in both respects. The way to deal with error, however, is by the use of careful evidence and straight reasoning. We can be sure that a large group is not misanthropic nor is it mentally incapable of sensible thought, so the bases of rational persuasion are available. The use of force, or even of ridicule, is in general illicit in dealing with groups. The believer in democracy, or even more basically a believer in the dignity of man, has a moral obligation to seek to remove differences of opinion among groups by honest argument.

I do not assert that there must be an element of truth in the position of every minority, and that we ought to sift out this element. There are minority views which I find mistaken—for example, the view that we should have protective tariffs for a large number of industries in the United States. But it is one thing to reject a view, and another to refuse to discuss in detail and in good humor the evidence on which it is held.

The issue of extremism is, so to speak, the extreme form of the problem of the debate between the liberals and the conservatives of America. Neither side seems to be able to understand the other's position. The greater part of the problem is that neither party seems really to understand the position of the other—to share the same fears, nurture the same hopes, or weigh the same evidence. It is as if there were a dialogue between two men, each of whom spoke the same words but with a different meaning. Let me try my hand as an interpreter. The discourse will be confined to economic issues.

Let us begin with the most fundamental issue posed by the increasing direction of economic life by the state: the preservation of the individual's liberty—liberty of speech, of occupation, of choice of home, of education.

The situation is presently this: everyone agrees that liberty is important and desirable; hardly anyone believes that any basic liberties are seriously infringed today. The conservatives believe that a continuation of the trend toward increasing political control over economic life will inevitably lead to a larger diminution of liberty. The liberals believe that this contingency is remote and avoidable. The more mischievous of the liberals point out that the conservatives have been talking of the planting of the seeds of destruction of liberty for decades—perhaps the seeds are infertile. Liberty is thus not a viable subject of controversy; neither side takes the issue seriously.

The lack of any sense of loss of liberty during the last two generations of rapidly increasing political control over economic life is of course not conclusive proof that we have preserved all our traditional liberty. Man has an astonishing ability to adjust to evil circumstances.

It is not possible for an observant man to deny that the restrictions on the actions of individuals have been increasing with the expansion of public control over our lives. I cannot build a house that displeases the building inspector. I cannot teach in the schools of the fifty states because I lack a license, although I can teach in their universities.

This list of controls over men can be multiplied many-fold, but it will not persuade the liberal that essential freedoms are declining. The liberal will point out that restrictions on one man may mean freedom for another. The building inspector who forces me to build in a certain way is protecting my neighbors from fire and pollution. The law that prevents me from teaching in a high school on balance keeps incompetents out of the class-room. The restrictions on one man, says the liberal, are a grant of freedom to another man.

Clearly the debate is unjoined—two groups are talking at cross-purposes. There is an issue, and it should be faced: has the past expansion of governmental controls diminished our liberties, and if so, which ones and how much? The burden is squarely on the conservatives. If they say that federal grants to education will lead to federal control of our schools, they ought to give some proof. What has happened in educational areas in which the federal government—or for that matter, the state—has long been acting? They say the farm program takes away a farmer's freedom of choice in occupation, and saps his initiative and independence. After thirty years of this program, some objective evidence ought to be available. The seeds-of-destruction talk is sheer indolence parading as prophecy.

A second striking failure of communication is the problem of individual welfare. The academic conservative is dedicated to an efficient price system. This price system will direct resources to their most important uses, weed out inefficient entrepreneurs, induce improvements in technology, and otherwise contribute to a large national product. Many so-called welfare programs inter-fere with the workings of this price system and are opposed by the conservative. A minimum wage law is a direct interference with this price system in the market for labor services, and wheat subsidies are a similar interference in the market for foodstuffs—and the conservative says both interferences should be stopped.

To the liberal the conservative's preoccupation with efficiency seems outrageous. The liberal sees a numerous family supported by an ill-paid wage earner, and asserts that an economy as rich as ours can afford to pay a meager $1.25 or $2.00 an hour to this wage-earner. The liberal saw a farm family bankrupted in 1933 by the collapse of our economy, and feels that no legitimate purpose is served by again subjecting farmers to hurricanes of economic adversity. A well-bred liberal will not openly voice his doubts of the benevolence of a conservative, but it is difficult to believe that the liberal does not suspect that the conservative has greater love for profits than for people.

I venture to assert that the conservative is an earnest friend of man but that he looks at welfare in a less personal and restricted way than the liberal. When the price of wheat is raised by a crop restriction scheme, everyone can observe the benefit to the owner of the farm, and it is this benefit that catches the liberal eye. The conservative is troubled by two other effects of the crop restriction scheme: a tax has been levied on all the consumers of bread; and the restriction scheme almost inevitably will lead to some waste of resources or, differently put, reduce the community's real income. These effects are obviously harmful to non-farmers. The conservative's opposition to minimum wage legislation is more direct: such legislation injures some of the lowest paid workers by forcing them into even lower paid occupations exempt from the act, one of which is unemployment.

The conservative's preference for low prices, strong incentives to diligence and thrift and inventiveness, and similar attributes of efficiency and progress, has indeed a substantial advantage over the liberal's plan of assisting particular needy groups. There are many, many needy groups in a society, and some take a generation or two or even three before they catch the eye of the liberal, be he reformer or politician. The liberal started to care for the poorly housed in American cities a few years ago. In the preceding 300 years the private enterprise economy had sole responsibility for improving their housing. The liberal hopes to take especially good care of the poverty-stricken in Appalachia in 1966—notice the date; but he will ignore the dozens of other groups of equal or greater need until someone publicizes their need. The conservative's programs are designed to help everyone, even groups too poor to have a press agent.

These remarks are intended to illustrate a general proposition: the conservative opposition to intervention by either government or private monopoly is commonly stated in efficiency terms but could always be restated in terms of welfare, and especially in the welfare of consumers. A conservative may be truly humane. It is fair to say that the conservative is compassionate for the great mass of the population which is moderately affected by each public policy, whereas the liberal is compassionate for the special, identifiable group which is most benefited or injured by the policy in question.

Here I am inclined to argue that the liberal should be asked to do more of the work in joining the parties to the debate. If the pebble of public policy sends ripples of harm out over the economy, they should certainly be reckoned in before deciding whether to cast the pebble. If, to do $50 of good in one place, we must do $30 or $70 of harm elsewhere, we ought at least to know about this harm.

But there is more than this to the conservative position. Suppose we wish to help a particular group of farmers or slum dwellers or a disaster-stricken community. Often it is possible—in fact, usually it is possible—to devise policies which impose a minimum of harm on other groups, or place this harm on a known group capable of bearing it. In our example of the farm program, for example, we can choose between direct income grants that do not lead to a waste of resources or—as at present—a crop restriction scheme that does waste resources. We can finance the benefits to farmers by charging more for bread, or by using general tax revenues. I may add that no economist who is outside active politics will defend the present farm program, whether he be liberal or conservative.

I shall be so absurdly fair-minded as to notice the reply to this discussion by a fair-minded liberal. True, he will say, too little attention has been devoted by us liberals to the effects of our policies on people who cannot afford to send a representative to the congressional committee hearings. We grant you conservatives humanity and shall reckon indirect effects of our policies henceforth. But do you deny that conservatives opposed social security, all farm programs, the urban renewal programs, the recent anti-poverty bill and so forth . . . ? Have not the conservatives been *too* preoccupied with the indirect and diffused costs of programs to give due weight to their direct and immediate benefits for hard-hit groups?

On reflection I am inclined to give two answers. The first is that the rise of per capita incomes (in 1964 prices) from about $500 in 1875 to $2,600 today is a measure of the immense benevolence implicit in a private enterprise system, and this rise has not only done more to eliminate poverty than all governmental policies ever devised, but has in fact also financed these policies. The second answer is, touché.

There are two issues concerning the competence of the state which divide the conservative and the liberal. One is the capacity of the state to withstand special interests; the other is its capacity to get things done. Roughly these issues amount to the questions:

does the state do things it should not, and does it fail to do the things it should?

Everyone will admit that the state enters fields simply because a politically well-situated group wishes assistance. The oil import quota system is attributable to only one argument: there are powerful representatives in Congress from the few states which have oil fields. Our tariff history is the same story many times retold. The continuance of the farm program on its present scale and scope is attributable only to the votes of farm areas. The list of such political ventures can be extended substantially.

The conservative argues that these programs reveal the vulnerability of the political process to exploitation by special groups. The vulnerability is greater, the greater the role of government in economic life: if the oil and textiles industries have been given import quotas, it is hard to deny quotas to meat (1964) and automobiles for Canada (1965). History suggests to the conservative that the way to combat these abuses is to have a self-denying ordinance: Congress must refuse to play the game of helping individual industries or localities.

The liberal's reply is two-fold. His lesser answer is that many of the programs are not so bad as all that: the farm program, for example, has not excluded all poor farmers from its list of beneficiaries. His larger answer is: we cannot refuse to use a weapon of public welfare simply because it is sometimes abused. We cannot abolish hammers because they are also used as blunt instruments.

The failure to join issues becomes obvious if we ask how we are to rid ourselves of policies which informed and disinterested people agree are undesirable policies. The conservative replies that we should make it hard to have any such policy: create (or rather, re-create) a persuasive tradition of nonintervention by Congress in the importation of individual goods, the pricing of particular goods, and so forth. The liberal replies that we must educate the majority of the population up to the level where they understand the objections to the undesirable policies and instruct their representatives to oppose them.

A professor can hardly deny the propriety of using education to achieve enlightened policies. Yet history does not suggest that it is a quick remedy for the abuses of special groups. The level of formal education of our population has been rising steadily for a century and it has reached historically unprecedented levels. There are probably more years of schooling in our population than world history recorded before 1925. If education of the public leads to lesser perversion of the political process by special groups, we should be able to detect this trend in legislation. The trend is painfully in the other direction: the special interest legislation has been on the rise throughout the twentieth century. The liberals owe it to themselves and to the society to start thinking about effective ways to contain the exercise of the state's economic power.

The second issue is the competence with which the state discharges its economic functions. Does regulation of railway rates keep them at proper levels? Does review of new stock issues protect the investor from loss? Does review of the truthfulness of advertisements protect consumers? Does the federal mediation service reduce the frequency or duration of strikes? Will the review of new drugs save human lives?

I ask you to believe a strange thing. No one knows the answer to questions of this sort. At most only a tiny set of policies have been studied with even moderate care. The conservative has not found it necessary to document his charges of failure, nor the liberal to document his claims of success.

The last subject of unjoined debate which I shall discuss is the question of the competence of the individual. The situation is this: the liberal finds the individual to be steadily losing the capacity to deal with the problems thrown up by an advancing industrial society. The consumer could once look at a horse's teeth, but how does he judge the quality of a motor car? The consumer once bought navy beans by the pound, but how does he know what is in the partially filled box of beans which also contains irium, or is it Pepsodent?

The conservative has several replies. One, which I shall merely note, is that even if liberals do not know how to buy an automobile, conservatives do. A second and more general response is that it is easy to exaggerate the difficulties. Even a non-mechanic can learn by the experience of his friends and of himself whether a given automobile manufacturer habitually makes reliable, durable, comfortable automobiles. And anyway, responsibility is good for a man.

This too is an unjoined issue, one that has a clear analogy to the question of the competence of the state. Take first that manly sentiment: a man should make his own decisions because this improves his character and induces him to enlarge his knowledge. This is both obviously true and plainly false. It does a man's character little good to be sold impure food, or to have his appendix removed by an incompetent doctor, or to be hit by a truck which has no brakes. On the other hand, if a man is allowed to make decisions only when unwise decisions are of no serious consequence, it is indeed hard to believe that experience will be much of a teacher.

The situation is complicated in practice by the differences among men in their ability to cope with given problems. Installment credit, for example, is a boon to the community at large: it permits men to improve the time pattern of their consumption. A few people, however, are hopelessly incompetent to resist the blandishments of salesmen, or even to understand the contracts into which they enter. How many such people must there be before credit sales are regulated to protect them—and, unfortunately, to make life more complex and expensive for the rest of the community?

The larger question of individual competence is really a very different one, however. It is, how well does our economy operate? That this is really the heart of the problem I hope to show by two examples.

The first concerns the sale of food in containers which convey an exaggerated impression of their contents: the partially empty box of a breakfast cereal. Suppose it is true that consumers do not weigh the contents or read the small print which contains this knowledge. There is another source of protection of the consumer: the rivals of the company which engages in this sort of packaging. If consumers buy the half-empty container at the same price as full containers, rivals will begin to lessen the contents and reduce the price—for of course their costs of production have fallen and they are eager to expand sales. This competition will continue until the price per unit of contents is what it was before the idea occurred. If people were as silly as the liberals say, corn flakes boxes would eventually be empty, but they would sell for the price of the cardboard.

In every case of the exploitation of the ignorance of consumers or workers or investors by a businessman, the leading protector of the exploited class is the businessman's competitors. I need not be well informed, because if anyone seeks to profit by my ignorance, his efforts will merely arouse his rivals to provide the commodity at a competitive price. Competition is the consumer's patron saint.

To be sure, competition does not always exist, and America has an antitrust policy precisely to combat monopolies and conspiracies of nominally independent companies. But the common complaint at the failure of the market to protect consumers and workers and investors is seldom directed to monopoly, but rather to the fact the the forces of competition do not exist, or are too weak, or act too slowly. The liberals have not done a good job of showing the profitability or the prevalence of fraud and deception. They have been content to rely upon scandalous incidents and a priori arguments. The defense of competition by the conservatives has also been too theoretical: the elegant economic theory which describes a competitive system has received entirely too little statistical elaboration.

There is a second resource of a non-expert in a complex world: he can hire an expert. If I want a reliable television set, I can purchase it from a reputable department store, one of whose main services is indeed to find good quality goods as my agent, and to guarantee their quality. If I want my son to get an education, I can hire a college to insure that his instructors are qualified. Our economy is simply plastered with institutions which specialize in providing knowledge, and in some fashion guarantee the accuracy of the knowledge.

The appearance of institutions supplying specialized information does not completely solve the information problem. My teacher, Frank H. Knight, used to say that in order to choose the best physician, a person would have to know how much medicine every physician knew, and if he knew that much, he would have sense enough to treat himself. How do I know that my department store is reliable, that the college will really go out and get good teachers?

I can't be *sure* of these things, just as I can't be *sure* a government agency will be staffed by competent men. But time is on my side. These specialized agencies have fairly long lives so I can judge them by results. Marshall Field and my university have been selling appliances and selecting professors for many years, so I can make a reasonably good prediction of how they will act in the years ahead. The reputation for rendering good service over long periods is the most priceless asset of a knowledge-supplying agency, and I can be sure that even dollar-chasing merchants and dollar-chasing college presidents will struggle hard to preserve this reputation.

These homely examples are not intended to answer the charge that the individual is losing the competence to make his own decisions. They are intended to suggest that a private enterprise economy has the powerful resources of specialization and competition to assist the consumer, the laborer, and the investor. New problems are constantly arising for the individual in modern society. The liberals have no right to assume that the individual is helpless in meeting them; the conservative has no right to assume that the market place will automatically protect the individual.

It is disturbing to look back upon these four grave issues: the preservation of liberty, the humanitarian treatment of the needy; the competence of the state, and the competence of the individual —and in each case observe a failure of the debaters to join issue. It is disturbing because both liberals and conservatives are honest, intelligent, and public-spirited. There are no villains in the picture. It is all the more disturbing that the good humor and good will of the participants to the debate are declining. The intellectual bears a heavy responsibility to restore cogency and mutual respect to the discussion.

The joining of the debate, and the collection and analysis of large amounts of the information I have called for, will not eliminate differences of opinion on public policy. We shall still have men disagreeing on the comparative roles of individual responsibility and social benevolence. No matter how we multiply our researches, there will be unresolved factual and theoretical questions which permit alternative policies to be followed. But an effective joining of the debate should put focus on our controversies and build progress into our policies. We need them.

For at least the past forty years the conservatives have been in
high alarm at the encroachments on liberty by the state. It would
be possible to amass a volume of ominous predictions—and not
by silly people—on the disappearance of individual freedom and
responsibility. Yet if we canvass the population, we shall find few
people who feel that their range of actions is seriously curtailed by
the state. This is no proof that the liberties of the individual are
unimpaired. The most exploited of individuals probably does not
feel the least bit exploited. The Negro lawyer who is refused
admission to a select club feels outraged whereas his grandfather
was probably a complaisant slave. But neither is complacency a
proof of growing tyranny. So let us look at what liberties, if any,
the typical American has lost in the recent decades of growing
political control over our lives. Let us face this American as he
completes his education and enters the labor force. Of what has
he been deprived?

Some additional barriers have been put in the way of entrance
into various occupations. Some barriers consist of the direct
prescription of types of training; for example, to teach in a public
school one must take certain pedagogical courses. More often,
the state imposes tests—as for doctors and lawyers and barbers
and taxi drivers—which in turn require certain types of training
in order to be passed. But few people consider such restrictions on
occupations to be invasions of personal liberty. The restrictions
may be unwise—those for school teachers are generally viewed as
such by the university world—but since the motive is (we shall
assume) the protection of users of the service, and since the
requirements are directed to competence even when they are
inefficient or inappropriate, no question of liberty seems involved. No one, we will be told, has a right to practice barbering
or medicine without obtaining the proper training. The freedom
of men to choose among occupations is a freedom contingent on
the willingness and ability to acquire the necessary competence.

The mentally and physically untalented man has no inherent right to pilot a commercial plane—or any other type of plane.

For consider: we surely do not say that a man born with weak or clumsy legs has been denied the portion of his liberty consisting of athletic occupations. At most a man is entitled to try to enter those callings which he can discharge at a level of skill which the community establishes. "Which the community establishes": the obverse of the choice of occupations is the choice of consumers. It can be said that the denial of my right to patronize lawyers or doctors with less preparation than the majority of my fellow citizens deem appropriate is the complementary invasion of my liberty. Why should the community establish the lowest levels of skill and training with which I satisfy my needs? The answer is, of course, that on the average, or at least in an appreciable fraction of cases, I am deemed incompetent to perform this task of setting standards of competence. I am, it is said, incapable of distinguishing a good surgeon from a butcher, a good lawyer from a fraud, a competent plumber from a bumbler, and so on.

Now, one could quarrel with both sides of this position: neither has my own incompetence been well demonstrated (especially when account is taken of my ability to buy guarantees of competence) nor has anyone established the ability of other judges to avoid mistakes or at least crudity of judgment. But these are questions of efficiency much more than of justice, so I put them aside not as unimportant but as temporarily irrelevant.

The real point is that the community at large does not think a man should have the right to make large mistakes as a consumer. The man who cannot buy drugs without a prescription does not really rebel at this indubitably expensive requirement. The man who is denied the services of a cheaper and less well-trained doctor or teacher does not feel that he has been seriously imposed upon.

The call to the ramparts of freedom is an unmeaning slogan in this area. If we were to press our typical American of age 22, he would tell us that some infringements on his liberties would be intolerable, but they would be political and social rather than economic: free speech should not be threatened—at least not by the first Senator McCarthy—and minorities should not be discriminated against. No economic regulation of consumers would elicit serious objection, and this younger person would often be prepared to go even farther in regulating consumers in areas such as health and education. We would have to propose policies remote from current discussion, such as compulsory location of families to hasten racial integration, before we should encounter serious resistance to public controls in principle.

Governmental expenditures have replaced private expenditures to a substantial degree, and this shift poses a related problem of liberty. The problem seems less pressing because private expenditures have increased in absolute amount even though public spending has risen in this century from perhaps 5 to 35 percent of income. Yet the shift has been real: we can no longer determine, as individuals, the research activities or dormitory construction of universities, the directions or amount of medical research, investments abroad, the housing of cities, the operation of employment exchanges, the amount of wheat or tobacco grown, or a hundred other economic activities. But again the typical American finds each of these activities worthwhile—meaning that he thinks that the activity will not be supported on an adequate scale by private persons.

On a closer view of things, some restrictions on individuals as workers will strike most Americans as unfair, especially if they are presented as indictments. Complaints will be aroused by a demonstration that political favorites have been enriched by governmental decisions which excluded honest competitors—and of course this can be demonstrated from time to time, or perhaps more often. The complaint, however, will involve equity much more than liberty.

This conclusion—that Americans do not think that the state presently or in the near future will impair the liberties that a man has a right to possess—is of course inevitable. It is merely another way of saying that our franchise is broad; our representatives will not pass laws to which most of us are opposed, or refuse to pass laws which most of us want. We have the political system we want.

The conservative, or the traditional liberal—or libertarian, or whatever we may call him—will surely concede this proposition in the large. He will say that this is precisely the problem of our times: to educate the typical American to the dangers of gradual loss of liberty. One would think that if liberty is so important that a statue is erected to her, then the demonstration that a moderate decline of personal freedom leads with high probability to tyranny would be available in paperback at every drugstore. Such a book is not so easy to find. In fact, it may not exist.

No one will dispute that there have been many tyrannies, and indeed it is at least as easy to find them in the twentieth century as in any other. Moreover, the loss of vital liberties does not take place in a single step, so one can truly say that a tyranny is entered by degrees. But one cannot easily reverse this truism and assert that some decrease in liberties will always lead to more, until basic liberties are lost. Alcoholics presumably increased their drinking gradually, but it is not true that everyone who drinks becomes an alcoholic.

The nearest approach to a demonstration that the tendency of state controls to increase beyond the limits consistent with liberty is found in Hayek's *Road to Serfdom*. But Hayek makes no attempt to prove that such a tendency exists, although there are allegations to this effect.[1] This profound study has two very different purposes: (1) A demonstration that *comprehensive* political control of economic life will reduce personal liberty (political and intellectual as well as economic) to a pathetic minimum. (I may observe, in passing, that this argument seems to me irresistible, and I know of no serious attempt to refute it. It will be accepted by almost every one who realizes the import of *comprehensive* controls.[2]) (2) If the expansion of control of economic life which has been under way in Britain, the United States, and other democratic western countries should continue long enough and far enough, the totalitarian system of Nazi Germany and Fascist Italy will eventually be reached. This second theme is not a historical proposition—and no historical evidence was given: it is the analytical proposition that totalitarian systems are an extreme form of, not a different type from, the democratic "welfare" states to which the book was addressed. Hayek was telling gentlemen drinkers, and especially some Englishmen—who were becoming heavy drinkers—not to become alcoholics.

The thirty-five years that have passed since the outbreak of World War II have seen further expansions of political control over economic life in the United States, and in most western European nations except Germany. Yet no serious diminution of liberties deemed important by the mass of educated (or uneducated) opinion has taken place. Another hundred years of governmental expansion at the pace of these recent decades would surely destroy our basic liberties, but what evidence is there that such an expansion will continue? Quite clearly, no such evidence has been assembled. But it is one thing to deny that evidence exists for the persistence of present trends to the point where they will endanger our liberties, and quite another to deny that such a momentum exists. Or, differently put, where is the evidence that we *won't* carry these political controls over economic life to a liberty-destroying stage?

This may be an impeccable debating point, but it will carry much less conviction than an empirical demonstration of the difficulty of stopping a trend. When men have projected the tendency of a society to a distant terminus, they have invariably committed two errors. The tendency develops in a larger number of directions than the prophet has discerned: no tendency is as single-minded as its observer believes it to be. And the tendency encounters in the society other and contradictory forces which eventually give the course of events a wholly different turn. We have no reason to believe that the current prophets are any wiser.

So I conclude: we should fish or cut bait. On the subject of liberty the conservative should either become silent or find something useful to say. I think there is something useful to say, and here is what it is.

The proof that there are dangers to the liberty and dignity of the individual in the present institutions must be that such liberties have already been impaired. If it can be shown that in important areas of economic life substantial and unnecessary invasions of personal freedom are already operative, the case for caution and restraint in invoking new political controls will acquire content and conviction. We cannot scare modern man with incantations, but we can frighten him with evidence. The evidence, I think, will take a variety of forms:

1. A full study of the barriers to entry in occupations, and of the extent to which the barriers can be defended on social grounds, will demonstrate, I believe, that the area of occupational freedom has been seriously restricted simply for reasons of

ignorance or special interest. If this is correct—if the present practices will not bear close review—then the danger of further extensions of such barriers will be substantially reduced.

2. The widespread belief in the incompetence of the individual and the efficacy of economic censorship of tastes is the second large area of potential invasion of personal freedom. This development has surely not benefited from close study: it has happened that errors of judgment or deficiencies of knowledge of a tiny fraction of consumers have led to restraints being imposed on all consumers, without even checking what gains are achieved by the censorship. My own study of the SEC [chap. 6], indeed, reveals a clear instance of where the gains are not worth the cost. If consumers are wiser than the public believes, and if political intervention is not infallible and economical, we shall be better able to stop future invasions of the consumer's freedom.

I do not know whether justice is more or less important than liberty, or whether they are even fully separable. The standards of justice under political direction of economic life, I conjecture, are deplorably low:

3. The state is now the giver of many valuable rights. The favorites get TV channels, or oil import quotas, or FDIC charters, or leases on federal grazing lands, or N.Y. state liquor store licenses, or waivers from the local zoning board. Who has studied the bases on which these favors are allotted? I suspect that a careful study would display vast caprice, much venality, and a considerable number of calluses on applicant's knees and navels. The harshness of competition may mellow somewhat in public repute when alternative systems of distributive justice are studied.

Studies of the types here proposed will, I am reasonably confident, give vitality and content and direction to fears for liberty in our society. But whether the studies confirm the need for reform and vigilance in preserving freedom, or suggest that such fears are premature, they are essential to remove this subject from the category of cliché. It is no service to liberty, or to conservatism, to continue to preach the imminent or eventual disappearance of freedom: let's learn what we're talking about.

TWO

The Traditional Regulatory Approach: The Absence of Evidence

The Tactics of Economic Reform

We are a well-meaning people. We are unanimously in favor of a healthy population, also fully employed, well housed, and deeply educated. To a man we wish prosperous and peaceful nations in the rest of the world, and possibly we are even more anxious that they be prosperous than that they be peaceable. We ooze benevolence, and practice much charity, and could easily become smug in our self-conscious virtue.

The denunciation of American complacency, however, is not my purpose, at least not my explicit purpose. I admire the humane and generous sympathies of our society—sympathies that extend now more than ever before to persons of all colors of skin, to the uneducated and the uncultured and the unenterprising and even the immoral as well as to the educated and the cultured and the enterprising and the moral. We are a people remarkably agreed on our basic goals, and they are goals which are thoroughly admirable even to one, like myself, who thinks one or two less fashionable goals deserve equal popularity.

Fortunately our agreement on basic goals does not preclude disagreement on the way best to approach these goals. If the right economic policies were so obvious as to defy responsible criticism, this would be an intolerably dull world. In fact I believe that each generation has an inescapable obligation to leave difficult problems for the next generation to solve—not only to spare that next generation boredom but also to give it an opportunity for greatness. The legacy of unsolved problems which my generation is bequeathing to the next generation, I may say, seems adequate and even sumptuous.

THE NEED FOR SKEPTICISM

It is not wholly correct to say that we are agreed upon what we want but are not agreed upon how to achieve it. When we get to

Reprinted from Graduate School of Business, University of Chicago, *Selected Papers*, no. 13 (1964).

specific goals, we shall find that our agreement does not always extend to orders of importance. For example, some people are willing to preserve personal freedom of choice for consumers even if the choice is exercised very unwisely in some cases, and others will be more concerned with (say) the health of consumers which these unwise choices may impair. Nevertheless, it is roughly true that we know where to go.

We do not know how to get there. This is my fundamental thesis: we do not know how to achieve a given end. We do not know the relationship between the public policies we adopt and the effects these policies were designed to achieve.

This surely sounds absurd: I am saying that although we have had a Securities and Exchange Commission for thirty years, we do not know how to improve the securities markets. I am saying that we have regulated the railroads for seventy-seven years [1964] and do not know how to achieve a sensible railroad rate structure. I am saying that no one knows whether a fair employment practices act will serve to reduce the discrimination against nonwhites in the labor markets. We can get on a bus labelled Economic Reform, but we don't know where it will take us.

You will find it hard to assimilate immediately a challenge to a belief which is so deeply implanted in you that it is simply self-evident. I am reminded of the equally formidable task undertaken in 1819 by a young English clergyman named Richard Whately. In a pamphlet with the title, *Historic Doubts Relative to Napoleon Buonaparte,* he argued that the evidence that Napoleon had ever existed was very unsatisfactory and inconclusive. He recognized, as I have just done, the difficulty of getting men to rethink an undisputed position.

> But is it in fact found that *undisputed* points are always such as have been the most carefully examined as to the evidence on which they rest? that facts or principles which are taken for granted, without controversy, as the common basis of opposite opinions, are always themselves established on sufficient grounds? On the contrary, is not any such fundamental point, from the very circumstance of its being taken for granted at once, and the attention drawn off to some other question, likely to be admitted on insufficient evidence, and the flaws in that evidence overlooked? Experience will teach us that such instances often occur: witness the

well-known anecdote of the Royal Society; to whom King
Charles II proposed as a question, whence it is that a vessel
of water receives no addition of weight from a live fish being
put into it, though it does, if the fish be dead. Various solu-
tions, of great ingenuity, were proposed, discussed, objected
to and defended; nor was it till they had been long
bewildered in the enquiry that it occurred to them to *try the
experiment*; by which they at once ascertained, that the
phenomenon which they were striving to account for, . . . had
no existence but in the invention of the witty monarch.

Whately's case against Napoleon's existence rested chiefly
upon the utter improbability of the man's career. As just one
instance,

Another peculiar circumstance in the history of this
extraordinary personage is, that when it is found convenient
to represent him as defeated, though he is by no means
defeated by halves, but involved in much more sudden and
total ruin than the personages of real history usually meet
with; yet, if it is thought fit he should be restored, it is done
as quickly and completely as if Merlin's rod had been
employed. He enters Russia with a prodigious army, which is
totally ruined by an unprecedented hard winter; (everything
relating to this man is *prodigious* and *unprecedented*;) yet in
a few months we find him entrusted with another great army
in Germany, which is also totally ruined at Leipsic; making,
inclusive of the Egyptian, the third great army thus totally
lost: yet the French are so good-natured as to furnish him
with another, sufficient to make a formidable stand in
France; he is however *conquered, and presented with the
sovereignty of Elba*; (surely, by the bye, some more *probable*
way might have been found of disposing of him, till again
wanted, than to place him thus on the very verge of his
ancient dominions;) thence he returns to France, where he is
received with open arms, and enabled to lose a fifth great
army at Waterloo; yet so eager were these people to be a sixth
time led to destruction, that it was found necessary to confine
him in an island some thousand miles off, and to quarter
foreign troops upon *them*, lest they should make an insur-
rection in his favour! Does any one believe all this, and yet
refuse to believe a miracle?

Whately was a young divine when he wrote this piece, which I interpret to assert that the evidence a typical Englishman possessed for Napoleon's existence was no better than the evidence he possessed for Biblical miracles.

I am jealous of Whately. He was arguing for miracles, which everyone wants to believe in, and in fact everyone wishes to benefit from miracles. Whately soon became an archbishop. I, on the contrary, am compelled to argue against miracles: for I assert that passing a law does not solve a problem. I shall be lucky if I am not fined for loitering on the highway of progress. But on with the task.

I doubt that I can use Whately's approach. One could indeed marvel at the credulity of reformers. In 1887 the railroads of this nation exceeded 180,000 miles, many times the length of the highways of the Roman Empire. The railroad lines and equipment had a value of perhaps 10 billions, or more than twice the expenditures of both sides on the Civil War. The railroads employed 700,000 men—itself the largest industrial army that history had ever seen. This stupendously vast empire was ruled by a set of entrepreneurs of great ability and utter determination. To establish an equitable rate structure, to govern this empire in the most minute detail, the Congress in its wisdom created the Interstate Commerce Commission. A committee of five men, aided by a staff of sixty-one and abetted by an appropriation of $149,000 (as of 1889) was to assume direction of the industry. Could anyone believe that this committee would change much the structure of rates, and not believe in miracles? But since you believe in miracles, I must part company with Whately.

When we undertake a policy reform or improve some part of the economy, there is one way, and only one way, to find out whether we have succeeded—to look and see. Now, only a naive person will believe that historical evidence is unambiguous. Some years ago a young man sued Columbia University, at which I was then professing, for a considerable sum of money because it had failed to teach him wisdom. The fact that he brought the suit was conclusive evidence of Columbia's failure. Nevertheless I agree with this befuddled ex-student that colleges should impart wisdom if they possibly can. I challenge anyone in the whole wide world, however, to prove that, on the average, colleges have taught wisdom, or that, on the average, they haven't. The burden of proof is too heavy for anyone to lift.

Still, it is easy to exaggerate the ambiguity of historical experience: after all, the past is the only source of knowledge of the future. Our trouble, frankly, is less that history speaks obscurely than that we have listened carelessly. We have not studied the experience of economic reform, and know not its successes nor its failures, its lessons on ways to proceed and ways to avoid.

And, of course, the past is instructive only if we study it. Suppose you are ill and I give you a medicine, chosen at random. You will probably survive and, since most medicines are not very potent, even get well. This is not too different from what medical research must be like, for all research involves the liberal use of trial and error. What turns this near-sighted groping into large progress is the recording of the outcome, so that recoveries due only to chance are separated from those due to the beneficial effects of a particular medicine. In a world without memory, there would be, not progress, but an endless succession of random moves, lacking any cumulative improvement.

So the results of experiment should be determined, and compiled. This may be Platitude No. 1 to the scientific investigator, but it is no platitude in the formulation of economic policy In political life it is an idea of considerable novelty, and there are those who would call it un-American except that it is also un-British and un-Russian and un-Indonesian.

Although we have studied the experience under some of our economic policies, the number and importance of those we have not studied are simply astounding. Let me give just three examples that will, I hope, suggest the problem we face in devising good policies for economic reform.

My first example is the regulation of rates for electricity, an area in which modern experimentation began in 1907 in New York and Wisconsin, and for which two-thirds of the states created special public service commissions as long ago as 1915. Yet when, in 1963, Claire Friedland and I began a study of the impact of these regulatory commissions on the level and structure of rates, we were the first investigators ever to do so on even a moderately comprehensive scale [chap. 5].

It was the implicit verdict of the many economists and political scientists who had studied the regulation of electrical rates during the last half century that a study of the effects of regulation was unnecessary. The bounteous literature implicitly asserts that the influence of the commissions on rates was obvious. The experts knew that of course regulatory bodies are not always competent or honest, but even so the experts were confident that on average the commissions hold down the prices below what the electrical companies would be able to charge because of their monopoly position in each community. If earlier experts could know that a dead fish weighs rather more than a live one, modern experts surely could know that a commission weights down electrical rates. But our study of the effects of regulation on rates came to the conclusion that the effects of regulation are apparently too small to be detected.

You may well find this conclusion incredible. How could hundreds of members of public service commissions have failed to discover long ago the futility of their labors, if they were of negligible import? Why do electrical utilities spend fortunes on lawyers to fight rate cases if they are setting the rates they wish? My ultimate answer is: look at the evidence. My immediate answers are: the efforts displayed by both regulators and industry are no greater than men usually display *pour le sport*; and if men never persist in what prove to be futile endeavors, why did not the American Indians capitulate by 1700?

A more recent economic reform was the creation of the Securities and Exchange Commission, some thirty years ago, to protect investors from the flamboyant falsehoods that on occasion appeared in the prospectuses that preceded new stock issues. The prospectuses which are now issued after much delay and very substantial expenditures have substituted grim statistics for the enticing loveliness of a seed catalogue. To what end?

Again my main point is that no one had studied the effects of this elaborate machinery on the fortunes of the buyers of new stock issues until I undertook to do so last year [1964, chap. 6]. Neither the security markets nor their regulators nor the academic economists have deemed it necessary to measure the undoubted beneficial effects of three decades of regulation.

Perhaps a word on how one measures the effects of regulation may be useful, for it is no simple task to disentangle one of many influences on the course of events. The SEC study illustrates one approach. Here I hypothetically bought every substantial new issue of industrial common stocks from 1923 to 1927, a period before the SEC, and from 1948 to 1955. The value of the stock in each of the five years following its issue was also ascertained. We can now calculate what happens to our new investment over time. There remains the problem of allowing for the considerable changes in this world between the reigns of Calvin Coolidge and Dwight Eisenhower. The differential effect of the SEC is measured by comparing values of these new investments with the outcome of buying established securities, over which the SEC has no significant control.

The main finding was that there was no important difference between the 1920s and the 1950s! I may add that it was fortunate that the purchases of new stocks were hypothetical: the investor in new issues of common stock lost twenty per cent of his shirt after two years in both periods.

My last instance is the effect of the Federal Reserve System on the stability of the American economy. This system of central banking was created fifty years ago and has controlled our money system ever since. Here economists have made studies of shorter episodes in the history of the sytem; it is widely accepted, for example, that the restrictive monetary policy of 1931–32 contributed greatly to the financial collapse of 1933. But my colleague, Milton Friedman, collaborating with Anna Schwartz, has recently published the first full-dress study of the effects of the Federal Reserve System upon the stability of prices and banking institutions throughout its history.

By now you may feel able to predict the results: that the Federal Reserve System has had no effect on monetary stability. But no—this time there was an effect:

> The stock of money shows larger fluctuations after 1914 than
> before 1914 and this is true even if the large wartime
> increases in the stock of money are excluded. The blind,
> undesigned, and quasi-automatic working of the gold stan-
> dard turned out to produce a greater measure of predic-
> tability and regularity than did deliberate and conscious
> control exercised within institutional arrangements intended
> to promote monetary stability (*A Monetary History of the
> United States, 1867–1960*, pp. 9–10.)

Many economists, and all bankers, will challenge Friedman's conclusions—in fact a fair number will challenge them even before they learn what he has written. But no one will be able in good conscience to say that Friedman's study was anticipated or has been contradicted by any other study of comparable scope and thoroughness.

Let me assume, tentatively and hopefully, that you are prepared to acknowledge that the relationship of policies to results is surprisingly obscure. I do not say that our knowledge is non-existent, because that statement would be distinguishably removed from truth. I do say our knowledge is extremely meager, and I wish now to pass on to you two questions which this deplorable state of affairs poses. First, why are we so poorly informed on the effective weapons of economic reform? Second, how shall we proceed with the reform of our economy?

The reasons we know so little of the effects of past economic policies are worth exploring briefly, because they tell us something about both scholars and political life. The studies that should have been made are the professional responsibility of economists and political scientists. I have no desire to criticize them. Economists are, by their own admission, learned, resourceful, diligent, and benevolent. Political scientists have accused themselves of similar traits. Why have these scholars failed to study much more intensively the relationship between public policies and the course of events? The main answers, I believe, are as follows.

The best scholars are not the best reformers. A scholar ought to be tolerably open-minded, unemotional, and rational. A reformer must promise paradise if his reform is adopted: a candid and qualified estimate of the effects of a given public policy would never arouse a majority from inertia. A reformer should have a low threshold of emotion: I am reminded of Samuel Plimsoll, of the ship line, whose sole stock in trade as a reformer, the *London Times* reported, was an unrivalled capacity for becoming fervidly indignant upon hearsay evidence. It follows that reformers care little for meticulous scholars—and use only those parts of the scholars' work which fit their needs—very much the way theatrical advertisements present selected adjectives from the reviews. The scholars are normally contemptuous of the reformers, whose scholarly attainments are indeed usually amateur. Reform and research seldom march arm in arm.

The economists have, until recently, been preoccupied with the workings of a comparatively unregulated economic system—what is loosely described as laissez-faire. They have seldom been in the forefront of economic reform—the two great exceptions being their advocacy of free international trade and policies designed to stabilize aggregate economic activity. They have had a marked preference for free-market organization of economic life.

The reformers, on the contrary, have seldom conceived of any method of achieving a given result except by giving explicit directions to individuals to act in the desired way. When a reform is not achieved by a given regulatory body, the reformers know no other solution than to give this or some other regulatory body more power and more instructions.

Economic reformers, moreover, have had one wondrous advantage for a century or more: the economy was improving in its performance in most ways, so most policies could claim success even if economic progress was quite unrelated to the reform. Some policies were designed to reduce poverty, but the Western economies were all becoming richer and poverty was diminishing as a result of economic growth. Other policies were designed to improve foods and homes, but technology was also striding forward here. Still other policies were designed to improve markets, but the advance of transportation and communication was also improving markets. It is as if the college dining room were to claim sole credit for the fact that seniors weigh more than freshmen.

If close study of the effects of previous reforms had been demanded by our political conscience, it would have been supplied in the past. There is an economic law, named after J. B. Say, to the effect that every offer of goods for sale is an implicit demand for the goods that will be received in exchange. Similarly there is a Say's law of scholarship: professors will study any problem that the society really believes in need of study. Our society has not believed that a close study of the process of economic reform is essential to devise effective reforms.

If I may be permitted to insert a refined advertisement, our long-run prospects for rational reform will be much improved as soon as our young people recognize the complexity of the problem. There is an absurd notion abroad that we mostly understand how our economy works and that a democracy—or, for that matter, a dictatorship—knows how to utilize the accumulated knowledge of the social sciences in legislation and administration. On the contrary, we are far from understanding either our economy or the ways in which to improve it, and the room for creative work in the social sciences is immense. If Mr. Nobel had been a wiser man, he would have directed his prizes to the social sciences to dramatize that really difficult goal of man, the achievement of a civilized society.

THE METHODS OF
EFFECTIVE REFORM

Now let me turn to what we should do, pending the vast research we need to inform our actions. We are a reforming society—we have been changing things incessantly since our founding—and we shall not suspend our discontents with economic life for a generation while scholars argue and computers hum. I suggest that we have failed to make anything like adequate use of the most powerful weapon of reform, and my final remarks are devoted to this weapon.

Reformers, I have remarked, are generally rather literal and direct-minded. If they wish to improve housing, they seek to have the state erect houses. If they wish to reduce accidents in factories, they pass a law against unfenced machinery. If they wish to help farmers to have remunerative prices, they pass a law which sets a minimum price. Yet we have seen that such policies are often unsuccessful.

The powerful weapon they overlook is the appeal to the self-interest of individuals. If incentives can be contrived to persuade people to act voluntarily to the goal of reform, we can be confident that our reforms will be crowned with success. Let me spell out and defend this bold claim.

That self-interest is a powerful drive is not really disputable. We recognize its strength so fully that we are not even conscious how much and how confidently we invoke it. Consider a very simple example. A progressive income tax—a tax taking higher percentages of larger incomes—is always reinforced by penalties on rich people who fail to pay their full tax obligations. But the progressivity would also be defeated if the less well-to-do tax-payers paid more than the tax the law demanded. You would think it odd, however, if I proposed that we impose severe penalties on those lower income families which overpaid their tax: quite aside from any other question, I would be assured that overpayment of income taxes was not a widespread problem in America. Or if I proposed a law prohibiting people from breaking into houses to contribute money to the tenants, I would be assured again that there really was no need for such legislation. We really know that self-interest is an extraordinarily powerful drive in man.

It may avoid useless controversy if I say at once two additional things about self-interest. First, it obviously is not the only force in man. Second, self-interest is not confined to a narrow egotism: the scholar who devotes a lifetime to arduous research is moved less by financial gains than by the respect and admiration of his fellow scholars—and if you doubt this, try publishing his work under your name.

Granted that self-interest is a powerful machine—how can we use it for economic reform? The answer is: by arranging that the people who are acting in a given area have incentives to act the way we wish. Let me elaborate this position through two examples.

The first example is the prevention of industrial accidents. If an accident occurs to a given worker, it will be due to one of four causes:

1. The employer has a dangerous place, so even careful workmen will have numerous accidents;

2. The fellow workers of the injured man have been negligent;

3. The injured worker himself has been negligent;

4. Everyone concerned has been careful but misfortune nevertheless occurred.

If we wish to reduce accidents, we may pass laws that machines must be fenced and workers must be careful, subject to penal sanctions. But we also reduce accidents if we put the costs of accidents partly or wholly on the people who prevent them. The employer should bear financial responsibility for the injuries due either to his operating a dangerous place, or to his maintaining an undisciplined shop in which fellow workers are allowed to be negligent. The injured worker should bear the costs of his own negligence.

Several hostile questions are immediately posed by this kind of use of financial incentives. Will not the employer flirt with bankruptcy to save a few dollars of expenses? Most employers dislike a finite chance of bankruptcy but we may require insurance, as indeed we now do with automobiles, which are also unfenced dangerous machines. Will not the worker ignore the costs to himself of negligence? Of course, especially after he has just mailed off a check for twice what he owes as income taxes. Suppose he is careless and injures himself—are we to allow his children to starve that he may learn a lesson?

This last question is more rhetorical than reasoned: in plain fact most injuries do not have major costs, and no children need be deprived of anything if a typical American worker loses a week's pay. But when major accidents occur, or the family is dreadfully poor, of course it should receive assistance. That a policy cannot work effectively in the extreme 1 percent of cases is no reason to eschew its help in the other 99 percent. Too often the argument is in effect that we should not paint the house because the paint will not protect the wood against artillery fire.

I have not studied the effect of financial responsibility upon accident rates in industry, nor has anyone else, so far as I know. Some partial use of incentives is in fact part of our system of workmen's compensation. I predict that where it has been employed it has been much more effective than direct regulation of safety practices. I predict this because the price system is so effective in directing men's energies in a thousand documented cases. I have, in short, a general theory to guide me in this area—a guide that the traditional reformer lacks.

My second example is racial discrimination in the labor market. I take this example because it is in the forefront of public discussion. It is in some ways a troublesome subject, but most reforms are.

The direct method of reducing discrimination in employment is to insist upon quotas of nonwhite workers, presumably proportional to their numbers. This is a most arbitrary standard: we cannot today staff one-tenth of the positions in theoretical physics, or for that matter in economics, with qualified nonwhites. It would be unfair, conversely, to hold them to only 10 percent of the best jobs in professional sports, which pay better than professorships of physics or economics. Moreover, the method of direct legislation—or other forms of direct social pressure—seems very unlikely to achieve important results: it works sporadically in time and capriciously in space.

The basic method of decreasing discrimination in the market is to offer a class of workers at bargain rates. This method has in fact been operative, and the large secular increase in the earnings of nonwhite relative to white workers has been due to the force of competition. The way we can best reinforce this trend is by increasing the financial incentives to employers to hire nonwhites.

We do this, not by increasing their wage rates—the market place will do this—but by increasing their skills. We have a distressingly large number of teenage nonwhites who are not in school or employed. I would favor a two-pronged movement to train them for employment at good wages:

1. A comprehensive program of tuition and support grants for teenagers (of any race) who wish to obtain vocational training in any craft at an accredited school. What we did for veterans after World War II out of gratitude we should do for our nonacademic teenagers out of compassion.

2. The removal of barriers to the employment of unskilled young workers at low wages while they are acquiring training on the job. These barriers include minimum wage rates and apprenticeship restrictions.

These latter proposals will not please some people: a fine thing, they will say, to raise the economic status of the nonwhite youth by lowering his wage rate to a dollar an hour. A fine thing indeed, I reply, to raise it from zero to a dollar.

The reduction of accidents and the elevation of the economic status of the nonwhite are admirable goals, we shall all agree. But there are reforms that some of us will wish and others will oppose.

An instance of a reform with debatable purposes is the maintenance of an import quota system on petroleum to protect the incomes of domestic crude petroleum producers. But let us accept this goal for the sake of argument, or more likely for the sake of election. Then the present system is capricious and arbitrary in high degree. It confers boons on particular importing companies proportional to the quotas assigned to them, and to which they have no claim other than that they used to import petroleum. The extent of these boons, and also of the benefits to domestic oil producers, varies with every change in supply and demand conditions either at home or abroad.

A simple old-fashioned tariff would escape all these objections, and provide a designated amount of benefit to domestic oil producers. The difference between foreign and domestic oil prices will accrue to the treasury instead of the importers, and the amount of this difference will be explicitly decided upon, not left to the whims of circumstance.

I choose this peculiar area of economic reform to show that the price system can be employed even for reforms of which many non-Texans do not approve. The price system can be used to achieve foolish as well as wise goals.

Effectiveness is a vast claim for the price system, but there may well be ruthless systems of direct control which are also effective. Two quite different considerations lead me to urge the use of the price system wherever possible.

The price system lays the cards face up on the table. Every policy benefits some people and imposes costs upon others; the fencing of machines is a cost borne by consumers of the product of the machine and a benefit to manufacturers of fences. (Paradoxically, it would require a complex analysis to determine whether workers are benefited.) With direct regulation these costs and benefits are neither measured nor located, whereas a price system displays them openly. If you believe in full disclosure at low cost, as I do, this is a great merit.

Finally, a system of reform that recognized the great diversity in men's desires and circumstances is both efficient and humane. The system of direct regulation cannot allow flexibility in the application to individual cases because favoritism cannot be distinguished from flexibility and diversity of conditions cannot be distinguished from caprice. The price system, however, possesses this remarkable power: if we make an activity expensive in order to reduce its practice, those who are most attached to the practice may still continue it. It is the system which excludes from an industry not those who arrived last but those who prize least the right to work in that industry. It is the system which builds roads by hiring men with an aptitude for roadbuilding, not by the corvée of compulsory labor.

CONCLUSION

Since I spent half of these pages lamenting over our disgraceful ignorance of the effects of past policies, it would seem proper to present concrete evidence of the effectiveness of the use of the price system that I have been supporting in the second half of these pages. It happens that such evidence exists, and in large quantities, but there is no third half of your time in which even to sample it. So hold to your skepticism and apply it equally to my allegations of proof: I have much more faith in the long run benefits of the practice of demanding evidence of the effects of various economic policies than I do in the beneficial effects of the policies that you or I now prefer. If we can bring ourselves to demand the credentials or effectiveness from the proposers of reforms, we shall reduce the charm of their calling but increase the welfare of our society.

4   The Economist and the State

In 1776 our venerable master offered clear and emphatic advice to his countrymen on the proper way to achieve economic prosperity. This advice was of course directed also to his countrymen in the American colonies, although at that very moment we were busily establishing what would now be called a major tax loophole. The main burden of Smith's advice, as you know, was that the conduct of economic affairs is best left to private citizens—that the state will be doing remarkably well if it succeeds in its unavoidable tasks of winning wars, preserving justice, and maintaining the various highways of commerce.

That was almost two centuries ago, and few modern economists would assign anything like so austere a role to the economic responsibilities of the state. The fact that most modern economists are as confident in prescribing a large economic role to the state as Smith was in denying such a role is not necessarily surprising: professional opinions sometimes change after 188 years, and economic and political institutions are of course even less durable.

But, surprising or not, the shifts in the predominant views of a profession on public policy pose a question which I wish to discuss. That question is: on what basis have economists felt themselves equipped to give useful advice on the proper functions of the state? By what methods did Smith and his disciples show the incapacity of the state in economic affairs? By what methods did later economists who favored state control of railroads, stock exchanges, wage rates and prices, farm output, and a thousand other things, prove that these were better directed or operated by the state? How does an economist acquire as much confidence in the wisdom of a policy of free trade or fiscal stabilization as he has

Presidential address delivered at the Seventy-Seventh Annual Meeting of the American Economic Association, Chicago, 29 December 1964. Reprinted by permission from the *American Economic Review*, March 1965.

in the law of diminishing returns or the profit-maximizing propensities of entrepreneurs?

The thought behind these questions is simple. Economists generally share the ruling values of their societies, but their professional competence does not consist in translating popular wishes into an awe-inspiring professional language. Their competence consists in understanding how an economic system works under alternative institutional frameworks. If they have anything of their own to contribute to the popular discussion of economic policy, it is some special understanding of the relationship between policies and results of policies.

The basic role of the scientist in public policy, therefore, is that of establishing the costs and benefits of alternative institutional arrangements. Smith had no professional right to advise England on the Navigations Acts unless he had evidence of their effects and the probable effects of their repeal. A modern economist has no professional right to advise the federal government to regulate or deregulate the railroads unless he has evidence of the effects of these policies.

This position, you must notice, is not quite the familiar one that an economist's value judgments have no scientific status— indeed I shall neither dispute nor praise value judgments. The position is rather that if a subject is capable of study, a scholar ought to study it before he advises legislators. Suppose you deplore disease or, conversely, that you greatly admire the much-persecuted germ. My assertion is that however you stand, you should not support proposals to compel or to forbid people to go to a doctor until you find out whether their attendance on a doctor will increase or decrease the incidence of disease. If this particular example strikes you as absurdly pedantic, I offer two responses. First, will your answer be the same whatever the state of medical science in a country? Second, we shall come to harder problems.

My task, then, is to ask in as hardheaded a way as possible what precisely was the evidence economists provided for their policy recommendations, evidence that successfully linked their proposals with the goals they were seeking to achieve. I begin with Adam.

I

Smith bases his proposals for economic policy upon two main positions. Neither basis is presented in a formal and systematic fashion, and there are serious problems in determining exactly why he wishes most economic life to be free of state regulation.

Smith's first basis for his economic policies was his belief in the efficiency of the system of natural liberty. There can be little doubt that this tough-minded Scotsman, this close friend of that cool and clear thinker, David Hume, had a deep attachment to the natural law of the late enlightenment. But Smith did not propose natural liberty as a lay religion of political life. Instead he argued, as a matter of demonstrable economic analysis, that the individual in seeking his own betterment will put his resourses where they yield the most to him, and that as a rule the resourses then yield the most to society. Where the individual does not know, or does not have the power to advance, his own interests, Smith feels remarkably free to have the state intervene.

Thus Smith says that to restrain people from entering voluntary transactions "is a manifest violation of that natural liberty which it is the proper business of law, not to infringe but to support"; yet he continues:

> But those exertions of the natural liberty of a few individuals, which might endanger the security of the whole society, are, and ought to be, restrained by the laws of all governments; of the most free, as well as of the most despotical. The obligation of building party walls, in order to prevent the communication of fire, is a violation of natural liberty, exactly of the same kind with the regulations of the banking trade which are here proposed. (*The Wealth of Nations* [Modern Library edition], p. 308)

Natural liberty seems to have been little more than a working rule, and Smith proposes numerous departures from natural liberty because the participants are incompetent or fail to consider external effects of their behavior.[1] He is quite willing to outlaw payment of wages in kind, which he believes will defraud the worker, and to put a limit on interest rates, because high interest rates encourage lenders to entrust their funds to improvident projectors, and to have a complicated tax system to change the uses of land.

The second foundation of Smith's strong preference for private economic activity was that he deeply distrusted the state. This distrust, I must emphasize, was primarily a distrust of the motives rather than of the competence of the state. Smith makes very little of inept governmental conduct—indeed he clearly believes that as far as efficiency is concerned, the joint stock companies, and even more the universities, are worse offenders than the state. His real complaint against the state is that it is the creature of organized, articulate, self-serving groups—above all, the merchants and the manufacturers. The legislature is directed less often by an extended view of the common good than by "the clamorous importunity of partial interests" (*Wealth of Nations*, p. 438).

Purely as a matter of professional appraisal, I would say that Smith displayed superb craftsmanship in supporting his first argument—that free individuals would use resources efficiently—but was excessively dogmatic in asserting his second argument, which accepted the competence but rejected the disinterest of the governmental machine. He gives no persuasive evidence that the state achieves the goals of its policies, and in particular he asserts rather than proves that the mercantile system had a large effect upon the allocation of British resources. Nor does he demonstrate that the state is normally the captive of "partial interests."

Smith's intellectual heirs did little to strengthen his case for laissez faire, except by that most irresistible of all the weapons of scholarship, infinite repetition. Yet they could have done so, and in two directions.

Where Smith finds the competitive market incapable of performing a task, they might have corrected him, for he was sometimes wrong. To a degree this was done: Smith's belief that the market set too low a value on investment in agriculture, and too high a value on foreign investment, was properly criticized by John Ramsay McCulloch (*Principles of Political Economy*, 1st ed. [London 1825], pp. 144 ff.), and the aberration on usury was of course promptly challenged by Bentham. But for each of Smith's errors that was corrected, several new ones were introduced. J. S.

Mill, for example, gravely argued that the competitive market was incapable of providing a reduction in the hours of work even if all the workers wished it—a mistake I am not inclined to excuse simply because so many later economists repeated it.

What I consider to be a more important weakness in Smith's position, however—his undocumented assumption that the state was efficient in achieving mistaken ends[2]—was not only accepted, but emphatically reaffirmed by his followers. James Mill's identification of the evils of government with the undemocratic control of its instruments was an extreme example, but an instructive and influential one. The holder of the power of government would always use it to further his own ends—so argued Mill with an oppressive show of logical rigor. It followed that only a democratically controlled state would seek the good of the entire public:

> The Community cannot have an interest opposite to its interest. To affirm this would be a contradiction in terms. The Community within itself, and with respect to itself, can have no sinister interest.... The Community may act wrong from mistake. To suppose that it could from design would be to suppose that human beings can wish their own misery. (*The Article on Government*—reprinted from the Supplement to the *Encyclopedia Britannica* [London 1829], p. 7.)

Hence a democracy, unlike a monarchy or an aristocracy, would do no unwise thing except in ignorance. And this exception for ignorance was not a serious one:

> There can be no doubt that the middle rank, which gives to science, to art, and to legislation itself, their most distinguished ornaments, and is the chief source of all that has exalted and refined human nature, is that portion of the Community of which, if the basis of Representation were ever so far extended, the opinion would ultimately decide. Of the people beneath them, a vast majority would be sure to be guided by their advice and example (Ibid., p. 32)

Education of the masses, and their instinctive reverence for the wisdom of their middle class leaders, those ornaments of society, would thus insure that the democratic state would seldom stray far from the public good. The argument meant that at the time the essay was written the American government was a reliable instrument of public welfare and fifty years later England's government would become so.[3]

It would be possible to document at length this proposition that the classical economists objected chiefly to *unwise* governmental intervention in economic life, but I shall give only two instructive examples.

The first example is provided by that fine Irish economist, Mountifort Longfield. Apropos of certain dubious programs to assist the laborer he wrote, "here Political Economy is merely a defensive science, which attempts to prevent the injudicious interference of speculative legislation" (*Lectures on Political Economy* [1834]). This sounds suitably conservative, but let us continue. Years later, as a witness before a Royal Commission on Railways, he complained that his timid fellow directors of the Great Southern and Western Railway underestimated the long-run elasticity of demand for rail service. To produce the necessary courage he proposed that the government appoint a director with unlimited power to vary the rates of each railroad, with the government taking half of any resulting profits and compensating all of any resulting losses.[4] Longfield wanted not laissez faire but half fare.

The second example is the major controversy provoked by the campaigns for the ten-hour day for women in factories, which reached success in 1847. This was one of the first of the modern English interventions in the contracts of competent adults, and it invited excommunication by the economic divines. This Factory Act was in fact opposed with vigor by two important economists, Torrens and Senior, but explicitly *not* as a violation of natural right. Torrens prefaced his criticism with a passage that reads better than it reasons:

> The principle of non-interference can be applicable to those circumstances only, in which interference would be productive of mischief; in all those cases in which the interference of the central authority in the transactions between man and man is capable of effecting good or averting evil, *laissez faire* is a criminal abandonment of the functions for the performance of which a central authority is established and maintained. (*A Letter to Lord Ashley* [London 1844], pp. 64–65)

Hence Torrens, and equally Senior (*Letters on the Factory Act* [London 1844]), criticized the ten-hour bill because it would lower weekly wages, increase production costs, and reduce employment by impairing the competitive position of the British textile industry abroad.

Both Senior and Torrens died in 1864, so they had adequate time, one would think, to have tested their predictions of the effects of the ten hour law. It is wholly characteristic of the insulation of discussions of policy from empirical evidence that no such study was undertaken by them, or by anyone else.

James Mill's oldest son, surprisingly enough, put up a stronger case against state control of economic life than his much more conservative father had. John Stuart did not follow his father in accepting the invariable wisdom of the democratic state, possibly because he was writing well after the Reform Act.[5] He rested the case much more on the defense of individual liberty, and fully three of the five reasons he gave for favoring laissez faire as a practical maxim were variations on the importance of the dignity, independence, self-reliance, and development of the individual (*Principles of Political Economy*, bk. 5, ch.11).

Although I reckon myself among the most fervent admirers of individualism, even for other people, I must concede that the younger Mill's position was ambiguous. He does not tell us how to determine whether a given public policy frees or inhibits individuals. Suppose I contemplate a program of public housing. If I bribe or force people into such housing, of course I have reduced their area of choice and responsibility. But I have also, I presumably hope, given a generation of children a chance to grow up in quarters that are not grossly unsanitary and inadequate for physical and moral health. Mill does not tell us whether this policy fosters or inhibits individualism—although I strongly suspect that he would have favored public housing, as he did free public education and limitation of hours of work for young people. If an economist is to be a moral philosopher, however—and I have do doubt that we would do this well too—he should develop his philosophy to a level where its implications for policy become a matter of logic rather than a vehicle for expressing personal tastes.[6]

Let us leap on to Marshall who brought up the rear of this

tradition as of so many others in English economics. He conceded an expanding potential role to the state, in the control of monopoly, in the housing of the poor, and in the treatment of poverty generally. Yet he persevered in his preference for private enterprise wherever possible. The preference rested heavily on the belief that bureaucratic management would be burdensome and inefficient (*Memorials of Alfred Marshall* [1925], pp. 274–76, 339 ff.; *Industry and Trade* [1919], pp. 666–72). Marshall at this point wrote the boldest sentence of his life:

> If Governmental control had supplanted that of private
> enterprise a hundred years ago [1807], there is good reason
> to suppose that our methods of manufacture now would be
> about as effective as they were fifty years ago, instead of
> being perhaps four or even six times as efficient as they were
> then. (*Memorials*, p. 338)

Yet the "good reason" was never presented, although it was more important to demonstrate this proposition if true than to answer any other question to which Marshall devoted a chapter or a book or even his life. Marshall's other reason for his distrust of government was the fear that Parliament would become the creature of special interests, and in particular the Trade Unions (*Official Papers by Alfred Marshall* [1926], pp. 395–96)—an unknowing but not unknowledgeable reversion to Adam Smith!

So much for a century of laissez faire. The main school of economic individualism had not produced even a respectable modicum of evidence that the state was incompetent to deal with detailed economic problems of any or all sorts. There was precious little evidence, indeed, that the state was unwise in its economic activities, unless one was prepared to accept as evidence selected corollaries of a general theory. The doctrine of nonintervention was powerful only so long and so far as men wished to obey.

II

There was no day on which economists ceased to commend reductions in the government's role in economic life and began to propose its expansion. The limitation of hours of work for children was supported well before the attack on the corn laws reached its climax. The statutes liberalizing dealings in property in the 1830s followed at a distance the regulation of passenger ships to protect emigrants.

How else could it be? The distinction between ancient police functions admitted by all and new regulatory functions proposed by some was most elusive. The same economist could and did repel the state with one hand and beckon it with the other.[7]

The expansion of public control over economic life which took place in the mid-nineteenth century in England, and a trifle later in the United States, was usually of this sort: a traditional state function was expanded or a new function was adopted which had close analogies to traditional functions. Economic effects were usually incidental to protective effects: the inspection of factories and mines, the sanitation laws for cities, the embryonic educational system, and most of the controls over railroads were of this sort (David Roberts, *Victorian Origins of the Welfare State* [New Haven: Yale University Press, 1960]; Oliver MacDonagh, *A Pattern of Government Growth, 1800–60* [London 1961]).

One thing did not change at all, however, from the heyday of laissez faire: no economist deemed it necessary to document his belief that the state could effectively discharge the new duties he proposed to give to it. The previous assertions of governmental incompetence were met only by counter assertion; the previous hopes of wiser uses of governmental powers by a democracy were deemed too prophetic to deserve the discourtesy of historical test. I shall illustrate this persistent neglect of empirical evidence with the writings of two economists who have almost nothing in common except great ability.

The first is Jevons. Governmental operation of an industry was appropriate, Jevons believed, if four conditions were fulfilled: (1) The work must be of an invariable and routine-like nature, so as to be performed according to fixed rules. (2) It must be performed under the public eye, or for the service of individuals, who will immediately detect and expose any failure or laxity. (3) There must be very little capital expenditure, so that each year's revenue and expense account shall represent, with approximate accuracy, the real commercial success of the undertaking. (4) The operations must be of such a kind that their union under one all-extensive

Government monopoly will lead to great advantage and economy (W. S. Jevons, *Methods of Social Reform* [London 1883], pp. 355, 279, 338). On what is this garbled description of a municipal water system based?—mature introspection, of course.

Jevons is equally devoted to the a priori method when he discusses public regulation. The "Principles of Industrial Legislation" are illustrated first with the problem posed by a dangerous machine. Neither worker nor employer, Jevons says, generally displays due concern for the dangers that lurk in the unfenced machine.

> But there remains one other mode of solving the question which is as simple as it is effective. The law may command that dangerous machinery shall be fenced, and the executive government may appoint inspectors to go round and prosecute such owners as disobey the law. (Jevons, *The State in Relation to Labour* [London 1882], p. 4)

Several aspects of Jevons' position are instructive. There is no showing of evidence on the failure of employers and employees to curb dangerous machinery. There is no showing of evidence that direct controls are simple and effective. Direct controls surely were not effective in factories too small to catch the inspector's eyes, and it is a completely open question whether they were effective elsewhere. And finally, Jevons does not conceive of the possible role of the price system in supplementing, if not replacing, direct inspection by a law making employers responsible for accidents. [8]

But let us recall who Jevons was; he was the economist whose supreme genius lay in his demand for empirical determination of theoretical relationships and his immense resourcefulness in making such determinations. This powerful instinct for empirical evidence spilled over into a proposal that wherever possible new policies should first be tried out at the local governmental level: "we cannot," he said, "really plan out social reforms upon theoretical grounds."[9] But, possible or not, he really so planned out his reforms.

We may learn how a theorist coped with the problem by

turning to my second economist, Pigou. In *Wealth and Welfare* (London 1912) he recited four reasons for distrusting the ability of legislatures to control monopolies. They were shallow reasons, but what is instructive is that all of them "can be, in great measure, obviated by the recently developed invention of 'Commissioners,' that is to say, bodies of men appointed by governmental authorities for the express purpose of industrial operation or control." Hence the government is now capable of "beneficial intervention in industries, under conditions which would not have justified such intervention in earlier times" (ibid., p. 250).

If time were not the most precious thing that one professor can give to another, I would follow in detail Pigou's travels from this inauspicious beginning. We would be instructed by the evidence which he found sufficient to a series of propositions on the state's competence:

> ... laws directly aimed at "maintaining competition" are practically certain to fail of their purpose. (p. 253)
> ... in respect of industries, where the quality of the output is of supreme importance and would, in private hands, be in danger of neglect, public operation is desirable. (p. 288)
> ... the relative inefficiency of public operation, as compared with private operation, is very large in highly speculative undertakings, and dwindles to nothing in respect of those where the speculative element is practically non-existent.[10]

The evidence, you will hardly need be reminded, consisted of a few quotations from books on municipal trading.

Pigou's views of the competence of the state were, like his predecessors' views, a tolerably random selection of the immediately previous views, warmed by hope. He felt that reliance upon such loose general reflections was unavoidable. On the question of whether public or private operation of an industry would be more efficient in production, we are told "at the outset, it must be made clear that attempts to conduct such a comparison by reference to statistics are fore-doomed to failure" (*Wealth and Welfare*, p. 274). How is it made clear? Very simply: by pointing out that it is unlikely that a public and a private enterprise operate under identical conditions of production. This test of the feasibility of statistical research would rule out all such research, and of course Pigou throughout his life accepted this implication.

Let me say that Pigou did not differ from his less illustrious colleagues in the superficiality of his judgments on the economic competence of the state—here he was at least as shrewd and circumspect as they. He differed only in writing more pages of economic analysis of fully professional quality than any other economist of the twentieth century.

Rather than sample other economists, I shall characterize more generally their role in the period of growing state control over economic life. The traditional and inevitable economic functions of the state such as taxation and the control of the monetary system are not considered in the following remarks. These functions pose no question of the desirability of state action and very different questions of the economist's role in policy. On the basis of a highly incomplete canvass of the literature, I propose three generalizations.

First, there was a large and growing range of policy issues which economists essentially ignored. If we examine the English legislation governing shop closing hours, or pure food and drug inspection, or municipal utilities, or railway and truck and ocean transportation, or the legal status of labor unions, or a host of other questions, we shall find that as a rule economists did not write on the issue, or appear before the Royal Commissions, or otherwise participate in the policy formulation. Before 1914 the detachment from contemporary policy was Olympian, therefore it was mortal but awesome. American economists, perhaps reflecting their Germanic training, were more interested in policy, so one can cite examples like John R. Commons on regulation of public utilities and on workmen's compensation laws, J. B. Clark and a host of others on the trust problem, and so on. Even here, however, many important economic policies were (and are still) ignored, among them pure food laws, wage legislation, fair employment practices acts, the zoning of land uses, and controls over the capital markets.

Second, even when economists took an active and direct interest in a policy issue, they did not make systematic empirical studies to establish the extent and nature of a problem or the probable efficiency of alternative methods of solving the problem.

It is difficult to support allegations about the absence of a given type of scientific work; often the allegation illuminates only the reading habits of its author. I am reasonably confident, however, that the following subjects were not investigated with even modest thoroughness: (1) the effects of regulation on the level and structure of prices or rates of public utilities; (2) the extent to which safety in production processes and purity in products are achieved by a competitive market and by a regulatory body; (3) the cost to the community of preventing failures of financial institutions by the route of suppressing competition compared with the costs by the route of insurance; (4) the effects of price support systems for distressed industries upon the distribution of income, as compared with alternative policies; and (5) the effects of policies designed to preserve competition. This list is short, but I submit that the examples are important enough to give credence to my generalization on the paucity of systematic empirical work on the techniques of economic policy. From 1776 to 1964 the chief instrument of empirical demonstration of the economic competence of the state has been the telling anecdote.

Third, the economist's influence upon the formulation of economic policy has usually been small. It has been small because he lacked special professional knowledge of the comparative competence of the state and of private enterprise. The economist could and did use his economic theory, and it cannot be denied that the economist's economic theory is better than everyone's else economic theory. But for reasons to which I shall immediately turn, economic theory has not been an adequate platform. Lacking real expertise, and lacking also evangelical ardor, the economist has had little influence upon the evolution of economic policy.

III

If economists have lacked a firm empirical basis for their policy views, one might expect that guidance could be derived from their theoretical systems. In fact, to the degree that a theoretical system has been submitted to a variety of empirical tests, it is a source of more reliable knowledge than an empirical uniformity in solitary confinement. The theory allows tests of the relationship incorporated in the theory that are outside the view of the discoverer of the theory, so these tests are more challenging.

The economists' policy views have in fact been much influenced by their theories. The vast preference for free international trade is surely based in good part upon the acceptance of the classical theory of comparative costs. The general presumption against direct regulation of prices by the state is surely attributable in good part to the belief in the optimum properties of a competitive price system. The growth of support among economists for public regulation of economic activities is at least partly due to the development of the theory of disharmonies between private and social costs, and partly also to the increasingly more rigorous standards of optimum economic performance.

If it would be wrong to deny a substantial influence of economic theory on economists' policy views, it would be wronger still to suggest that the policies follow closely and unambiguously from the general theory. Our first example of free trade will suffice to illustrate the looseness of the connection. Smith supported free trade because he believed that tariffs simply diverted resources from more productive to less productive fields, and the absence of an explanation for the rates of exchange between foreign and domestic commodities did not bother him. A century later Sidgwick argued that on theoretical grounds tariffs were often beneficial to a nation, but that "from the difficulty of securing in any actual government sufficient wisdom, strength, and singleness of aim to introduce protection only so far as it is advantageous to the community" the statesman should avoid protective duties (*Principles of Political Economy* [London 1883], pp. 485–86). To the extent that theory was guiding Sidgwick, surely it was a theory of government rather than of economics.

There is one primary reason why the theory is not, as a rule, coercive with respect to the policies that a believer in the theory must accept: a theory can usually be made to support diverse policy positions. Theories present general relationships, and which part of a theory is decisive in a particular context is a matter of empirical evidence. Consider the wages-fund doctrine, if I may be permitted to refer to it without its almost inseparable prefix, notorious. This theory asserted that there was a relatively fixed amount to be paid in wages in the short run, and that if one group got higher wages, other groups would get lower wages or be unemployed. It followed that if a particular group of workers formed a union and managed to raise their wages, other workers would bear the burden, and numerous disciples of the wages-fund doctrine accepted this policy view. (For example, J. E. Cairnes, *Some Leading Principles of Political Economy* [London 1873], pp. 258–60). But John Stuart Mill could argue, quite in the opposite direction, that since most workers would be at a subsistence level, at most the successful union would inflict only short-run harm on other workers, whereas its higher income could be permanent. (*Principles of Political Economy*, Ashley ed. [London 1929], p. 402). And obviously it is a quantitative question whether the short-run costs or the permanent benefits were larger.

What is true of the wages-fund theory is true of other theories: an empirical question always insists upon intruding between the formal doctrine and its concrete application. The truly remarkable fact is not that economists accepting the same theory sometimes differ on policy, but that they differ so seldom. The wide consensus at any time comes, I suspect, from a tacit acceptance of the same implicit empirical assumptions by most economists. All classical economists accepted as a fact the belief that wage earners would not save, although they had no evidence on the matter. All modern economists believe that they will never encounter Edgeworth's taxation paradox, with no more evidence. All economists at all times accept the universality of negatively sloping demand curves, and they do so without any serious search for contrary empirical evidence.

These empirical consensuses have no doubt usually been correct—one can know a thing without a sophisticated study. Truth was born before modern statistics. Yet generations of economists also believed that over long periods diminishing returns would inevitably triumph over technological advance in agriculture, a view that agricultural history of the last 100 years has coolly ignored.

A second and lesser source of the loose connection between theory and policy has been the difficulty of translating theory into policy because of practical politics or administration. The economist refrains from drawing a policy conclusion because its implementation would pose large social or administrative costs. Mill dismissed an income tax because of the inquisitorial burdens it would put on taxpayers; one would have thought that he would remember that an earlier inquisition had been welcomed to Spain. For at least 100 years economists have recommended that a nation proceed to free trade gradually over a five-year period to ease the transition, and the period is usually lengthened if protectionism is on the ascendant. I have often wondered why we deem it necessary to tell a confirmed drunkard not to reduce his drinking too rapidly.

A third, and fortunately a moderately rare, reason for separating theory from policy is flagrant inconsistency, usually stemming from that great source of inconsistency in intelligent men, a warm heart. Marshall proved—rather unconvincingly, I must say—that the doctrine of consumer surplus instructed us to tax necessaries rather than luxuries (Alfred Marshall, *Principles of Political Economy*, 8th ed. [London 1920], p. 467 n.). The idea was disposed of in a footnote because it disregarded ability to pay. The economic arguments against minimum wage legislation have usually been refuted by reference to the need of poorer people for larger incomes.

The essential ambiguity of general theoretical systems with respect to public policy, however, has been the real basis of our troubles. So long as a competent economist can bend the existing theory to either side of most viable controversies without violating the rules of professional work, the voice of the economist must be a whisper in the legislative halls.

IV

The economic role of the state has managed to hold the attention of scholars for over two centuries without arousing their curiosity. This judgment that the perennial debate has refused to leave the terrain of abstract discourse is true, I believe, of the continental literature as well as the English and American literature. Economists have refused either to leave the problem alone or to work on it.

Why have not the effects of the regulatory bodies on prices and rates been ascertained, even at the cost of a 1 percent reduction in the literature on how to value assets for rate purposes? Why have not the effects of welfare activities on the distribution of income been determined for an important range of such activities, even at the cost of a 1 percent reduction in denunciations of the invasion of personal liberty? Why has not the degree of success of governments in bringing private and social costs together been estimated, even at the cost of a 1 percent reduction in the literature on consumer surplus? Why have we been content to leave the problem of policy unstudied?

This variously phrased question can be considered to be a request for either a formal theory of state action or a set of empirical studies of the comparative advantages of public and private control.

Consider first the control over economic life as a formal theoretical problem. Why do we not have a theory to guide us in ascertaining the areas of comparative advantage of uncontrolled private enterprise, competitive private enterprise, public regulation, public operation, and the other forms of economic organization? This theory would predict the manner in which the state would conduct various economic activities, such as protecting consumers from monopoly or fraud, assisting distressed industries and areas, or stimulating inventions. The theory might yield rules such as that a competitive system is superior for introducing new products, or public enterprise is superior where there are many parties to a single transaction. That we have not done so is attributable, I conjecture, to two difficulties.

The first difficulty is that the issue of public control had a constantly changing focus: it was the relations of labor and employers one year, the compensation to tenants for improvements on farms and the control of railroad rates the year thereafter. At any one time few areas of economic life were seriously in dispute: most economic activities were uncontroversially private or public. That a single theory should be contrived to guide society in dealing with these various and changing problems was perhaps too great an abstraction to encourage serious efforts.

Moreover, and this is the second difficulty, the standard apparatus of the economist is not clearly appropriate. Ordinary maximizing behavior, with the ordinary rewards and obstacles of economic analysis, does not seem directly applicable to the problem. The bounds of state competence, and the areas of its superiority over variously controlled private action, are difficult to bring within a coherent theoretical system.

In short, the theory of public policy may be a difficult theory to devise, although until we have tried to devise it even this opinion is uncertain.

A usable theory of social control of economic life was not essential, however, to professional study of policy: could not the economist make empirical studies of the effects of various ways of dealing with specific problems? The state regulates machinery in factories: does this reduce accidents appreciably? The state regulated the carriage of emigrants from England and Ireland to the new world—what did the regulations achieve? A thousand prices had been regulated—were they lower or stickier than unregulated prices? The empirical answers would obviously have contributed both to public policy and to the development of a general theory of public and private economy.

Here we must pause, not without embarrassment, to notice that we could ask for empirical studies in areas traditional to economics as well as in the netherland of half economics, half political science. We need not be surprised, I suppose, that we know little of the effects of state regulation, when we also know very little about how oligopolists behave. Marshall's theory that the differences between short- and long-run prices and profits are regulated by the differences between short- and long-run reactions of supply will be 75 years old next year [1964]. Despite its immense influence, this theory has yet to receive a full empirical test. If such basic components of modern economic theory have escaped tests for quantitative significance, it is hardly surprising that our antitrust laws, our motor carrier regulation, and our control of insurance company investments have also escaped such tests.

Still, there has been a difference. Empirical tests of economic theories have been made for generations, and with greater frequency and diligence than we encounter in the area of social experiments. Already in 1863 Jevons had ascertained the serious fall in the value of gold consequent upon the Californian and Australian gold discoveries—it was 26 percent over the 13-year period, 1849-62. No such diligence or ingenuity can be found in the study of state controls at that time. A half century later Henry Moore was calculating statistical demand curves; again the study of the effects of public policies was lagging.

The age of quantification is now full upon us. We are now

armed with a bulging arsenal of techniques of quantitative analysis, and of a power—as compared to untrained common sense—comparable to the displacement of archers by cannon. But this is much less a cause than a consequence of a more basic development: the desire to measure economic phenomena is now in the ascendant. It is becoming the basic article of work as well as of faith of the modern economist that at a minimum one must establish orders of magnitude, and preferably one should ascertain the actual shapes of economic functions with tolerable accuracy.

The growth of empirical estimation of economic relationships, please notice, did not come as a response to the assault on formal theory by the German Historical School, nor was it a reply to the denunciations of theory by the American Institutionalists. It has been a slow development, contributed to by an earlier development in some natural sciences but mostly by the demonstrated successes of the pioneers of the quantitative method—the Jevons, the Mitchells, the Moores, the Fishers.

It is a scientific revolution of the very first magnitude—indeed I consider the so-called theoretical revolutions of a Ricardo, a Jevons, or a Keynes to have been minor revisions compared to the vast implications of the growing insistence upon quantification. I am convinced that economics is finally at the threshold of its golden age—nay, we already have one foot through the door.

The revolution in our thinking has begun to reach public policy, and soon it will make irresistible demands upon us. It will become inconceivable that the margin requirements on securities markets will be altered once a year without knowing whether they have even a modest effect. It will become impossible for an import-quota system to evade the calculus of gains and costs. It will become an occasion for humorous nostalgia when arguments for private and public performance of a given economic activity are conducted by reference to the phrase, external economies, or by recourse to a theorem on perfect competition.

This is prophecy, not preaching. You have listened to sage advice on what to study and how to study it for well over a century. If you had heeded this advice, you would have accomplished almost nothing, but you would have worked on an immense range of subjects and with a stunning array of approaches. Fortunately you have learned that although such advice is almost inevitable on such occasions as the retirement of an officer of a professional society, it is worth heeding only when it is backed by successful examples. I have no reason to believe that you left your tough-mindedness at home tonight, and I shall respect it. I assert, not that we should make the studies I wish for, but that no one can delay their coming.

I would gloat for one final moment over the pleasant prospects of our discipline. That we are good theorists is not open to dispute: for 200 years our analytical system has been growing in precision, clarity, and generality, although not always in lucidity. The historical evidence that we are becoming good empirical workers is less extensive, but the last half-century of economics certifies the immense increase in the power, the care, and the courage of our quantitative researches. Our expanding theoretical and empirical studies will inevitably and irresistibly enter into the subject of public policy, and we shall develop a body of knowledge essential to intelligent policy formulation. And then, quite frankly, I hope that we become the ornaments of democratic society whose opinions on economic policy shall prevail.

THREE

The Traditional Regulatory Approach: Some Evidence

5

What Can Regulators Regulate?: The Case of Electricity

(In Collaboration with
Claire Friedland)

The literature of public regulation is so vast that it must touch on everything, but it touches seldom and lightly on the most basic question one can ask about regulation: does it make a difference in the behavior of an industry? This impertinent question will strike anyone connected with a regulated industry as palpably trivial. Are not important prices regulated? Are not the routes of a trucker and an airline prescribed? Is not entry into public utility industries limited? Is not an endless procession of administrative proceedings aging entrepreneurs and enriching lawyers?

But the innumerable regulatory actions are conclusive proof, not of effective regulation, but of the desire to regulate. And if wishes were horses, one would buy stock in a harness factory.

The question of the influence of regulation can never be answered by an enumeration of regulatory policies. A thousand statutes now forbid us to do things that we would not dream of doing even if the statutes were repealed: we would not slay our neighbor, or starve our children, or burn our house for the insurance, or erect an abattoir in the back yard. Whether the statutes really have an appreciable effect on actual behavior can only be determined by examining the behavior of people not subject to the statutes.

An order to a trucker not to haul goods between cities A and B is even more difficult to assess. He may not wish to have this route, in analogy to the laws governing our personal behavior. But let him wish with all his heart to have it, and be denied; there still will be no economic effect of the regulation if others are allowed, in adequate number, to have the desired route.

The point at issue may be restated in the language of economics. An industry's output and price are normally governed primarily by the basic economic and technological determinants of supply and demand: by whether the demand curve is D_1 or D_2,

Reprinted by permission from the *Journal of Law and Economics* 5 (October 1962).

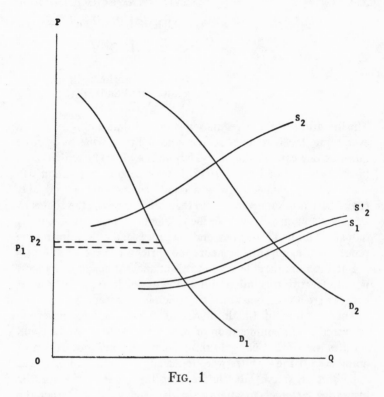

FIG. 1

and the supply curve is S_1 or S_2 (see fig. 1). Regulation will affect price and output only if it shifts the curves or the point on a curve where the industry operates. Does regulation introduce shifts in curves of the magnitude of S_1 to S_2 or S_1 to S'_2? In the latter event its effect will be negligible. Does regulation shift the effective operating point from p_1 to p_2? Then its effect will again be negligible.

The test of the economic effect of regulation is essentially independent of the content of the formal regulations. No degree of care in analyzing the regulations, or even their administration, will tell us whether they rubber-stamp or slightly heckle the state of affairs or substantially alter it.

What does one mean in saying that regulation has had large or small effects? He means that of the observed economic behavior in a certain industrial sector, a large or small part can be explained only by recourse to regulation. Consider these examples:

1. Is the decline of railroading due in any important part to ICC regulations? If in other economies with rising incomes and extensive adoption of automobiles and trucks the railroad traffic shows a pattern similar to ours, then regulation has not been the primary influence.

2. Do utility commissions reduce the differential in prices of utility services to large and small buyers? If in a group of unregulated markets we observe a mean ratio of rates of large to small buyers of m_{nr}, and in regulated markets a ratio of m_r, do m_{nr} and m_r differ significantly? If of the total variance among markets in the ratio of rates of large to small buyers only 2 percent can be explained by regulation, the regulations have negligible impact.

3. Do regulatory bodies succeed in preventing monopoly profits? We take it that they will usually prevent such profits from appearing explicitly in accounting statements. Whether they go beyond this may be judged, for example, by the fortunes of investors in stocks of regulated companies over periods extending from pre-regulation on, compared with those of investors in similar but unregulated enterprises.

These summary remarks will deceive no informed person as to the analytical and empirical complexity of the task of isolating the effects of regulation. They are intended only to suggest why one does not read the regulations to reach the answer.

We propose now to make an investigation of one regulated industry to explore techniques and hopefully reach tentative results. This is the electric utility industry. Here we face three major problems: (1) What firms are regulated? (2) What effects of regulation shall we study, and how shall we measure them? (3) How do we explain our findings?

WHEN IS A FIRM REGULATED?

Every enterprise producing and distributing electricity has been regulated since its founding by way of charter limitations and franchises; its use of public thoroughfares was enough to insure this. It would therefore be possible to say that there is no unregulated sector to provide a base for judging the effects of regulation. This statement would not be acceptable to the professional writers on public utilities: they hail the beginnings of effective regulation with the establishment of the public service

commissions in New York and Wisconsin in 1907 (L. S. Lyon and
V. Abramson, *Government and Economic Life* 636 [1940]; Twentieth Cent. Fund, *Electric Power and Government Policy* 65, 235
[1948]). Yet these specialists have assuredly not faced the problem of measuring the effects of regulation, so their judgments are
suspect. Indeed, if we accepted their judgments our problem
would be solved, for they never question the importance of
(effective!) regulation.

There is no substitute for an objective measure of regulation,
and the one we choose is the creation of a special state commission endowed with the power to regulate rates of electric utilities.[1]
It may be complained that some of these commissions were long
ineffective, or that municipal regulation was effective earlier in
some states. Such assertions can only be tested by a study invoking
another criterion of the existence of regulation: the year the
commission issued its first rate order upheld by the courts, the
year the commission first spent $100,000 or published 100 pages
of orders, and so forth. But it is intrinsic to the problem that there
be an independent criterion of regulation, and that findings on
effectiveness be conditional on acceptance of that criterion.
There is a strict analogy with the problem of estimating the
influence of monopoly, where the result is conditioned by the
criterion of monopoly (concentration ratio, number of firms, etc.).

The classification of states by the existence of regulatory
commissions with jurisdiction over electric utilities is given in
table A1 in the appendix [to this chapter]. The beginning of
regulation by this criterion varied as shown in the accompanying
tabulation. Two-thirds of the states had commissions by 1915,
three-quarters by 1922.

	States
Before 1910	6
1910–20	29
1920–30	1
1930–40	3
1940–50	2
1950–60	2

THE EFFECTS OF REGULATION
ON RATES AND RETURNS

There are two basic purposes of the public regulation of prices:

the curtailment of the exercise of monopoly power and the elimination of certain forms of price discrimination. There will no doubt be other effects on prices, including unintended effects such as the short term rigidity of price commonly associated with regulation, but we shall concentrate upon these basic purposes. Our analysis of effects will be limited to the period up to 1937, simply because by that time 39 states had regulating commissions. By that date every unregulated state had at least two adjoining states with regulatory commissions, and even a showing of no difference in rates thereafter would be ambiguous: it could be argued that the threat of regulation was always latent in the unregulated states. This position does not seem wholly convincing to us—in a sense the threat of regulation was operative as soon as the Interstate Commerce Commission was created —but the small number of unregulated states after 1937 offers statistical support for this terminus.

The Level of Rates

We shall make little use of the direct comparison of the average level of rates in regulated and unregulated states, of which a sample summary is given in table 1.[2] The ambiguity of simple differences may be illustrated by the data for 1917. In this year the average revenue per KWH was 1.88 cents in regulated states and 3.20 cents in unregulated states, which might suggest that regulation lowered rates by almost 40 percent. But we can classify the rates of these states in several ways (see table 2). This classification makes clear the fact that rates were lower on average

TABLE 1

AVERAGE REVENUE PER KWH, STATES WITH AND
WITHOUT REGULATION, 1912-37

YEAR	REGULATED[*]		UNREGULATED	
	States	Revenue (Cents)	States	Revenue (Cents)
1912.......	6	2.30	41	2.99
1917.......	31	1.88	16	3.20
1922.......	33	2.44	12	3.87
1927.......	35	2.85	10	4.21
1932.......	34	2.91	8	3.69
1937.......	34	2.32	6	3.04

[*]A state is considered regulated in a given year if commission regulation was established three years previously.

TABLE 2

	NUMBER OF STATES	AVERAGE RATE		
		1917	1912	1907
States instituting regulation before 1912.........	6	1.88	2.30	2.76
States instituting regulation from 1912 to 1917...	25	1.88	2.30	2.93
States not regulating before 1917...................	16	3.20	4.07	4.34

in the regulating states, not only *after* but also *before* regulation.

The basic fact is, of course, that regulation is associated with economic characteristics which also exert direct, independent influences on rates—the size and urbanization of the population, the extent of industrialization, etc. To isolate the effects of regulation we must take direct account of these economic factors. We do so by the following procedure.

The main determinants of the level of rates for an unregulated monopolist are assumed to be the size of the market and its density (which affect both production and distribution costs), the price of fuel, and the incomes of consumers. We approximate the market size and density by the population in cities with 25,000 or more population; the fuel costs by an equivalent BTU cost and by the proportion of power derived from hydroelectric sources; and consumer incomes by per capita state income. We fit the equation,

$$\log p = a + b \log U + c \log p_F + dH + e \log Y + fR,$$

where

p = average revenue per KWH, in cents;

U = population in cities over 25,000 (in thousands);

p_F = price of fuel (in dollars per BTU equivalent ton of bituminous coal);

H = proportion of power from hydroelectric sources;

Y = per capita state income, in dollars;

R = dummy variable, 0 if an unregulated state, 1 if a regulated state.

The results of fitting this equation to 1922 data are presented in table 3. The regression of millions of KW's of output, in logarithms, on these variables is also added.

The effects of regulation may be expressed in two ways: by the regression coefficient of the dummy variable representing regulation or by the difference in the coefficient of multiple determination including and excluding regulation. By either standard, regulation had no effect upon the level of rates in 1922.

For the other census years we use the abbreviated regression equations summarized in table 4. No effect of regulation is observable through 1932. The 1937 equation does display a regulation effect, but it is localized in the sales to commercial and industrial consumers—the class of consumers that regulation was *not* designed to protect. We believe even this modest 1937 effect would be eliminated by a fuller statistical analysis.[3]

We conclude that no effect of regulation can be found in the average level of rates.

The Rate Structure

We have examined two aspects of the rate structure for possible influences of regulation. The first is the ratio of monthly bills of domestic consumers for larger amounts of electricity relative to smaller amounts. Here our expectation was that the regulatory bodies would recognize the greater potential political popularity of low rates for the numerous consumers who buy small quantities. The evidence is essentially negative (table 5): in only one of four comparisons was the ratio of monthly bills significantly different in regulated states from unregulated states.[4] The quantity rate structure for domestic consumers seems independent of the existence of regulation.

A second aspect of the rate structure where regulation might be expected to be influential is in the comparative charges to domestic and industrial buyers. The regulatory bodies would reduce domestic rates relative in industrial rates if they sought to reduce discrimination; the industrial users presumably have better alternative power sources and therefore more elastic demands. Or, again as a political matter, the numerous domestic users might be favored relative to the industrial users. To test this expectation, the average ratio of charges per KWH to domestic users to charges to industrial users was calculated for two years

TABLE 3

REGRESSION EQUATIONS OF AVERAGE REVENUE PER KWH AND OUTPUT ON URBAN POPULATION, COST OF FUEL, PER CAPITA INCOME, PROPORTION OF HP FROM HYDROELECTRIC, AND REGULATION, 47 STATES, 1922

DEPENDENT VARIABLE	CONSTANT TERM	REGRESSION COEFFICIENTS AND THEIR STANDARD ERRORS					R^2	
		Urban Population	Cost of Fuel	Per Capita Income*	Proportion of HP from Hydroelectric	Regulation	Including Regulation	Excluding Regulation
Average revenue per KWH.......	.0918	-.0592* (.0248)	.0604 (.1665)	.230 (.204)	-.498 (.083)	-.0109 (.0068)	.567	.540
Output...........	-.166	.395 (.052)	-.577 (.349)	.718 (.428)	.491 (.174)	.0172 (.0143)	.694	.684

*Linear interpolations between averages are for the following years: 1919-21--Source: Maurice Leven, Income in the Various States (1925); 1929-31--Source: U.S. Office of Business Economics, Personal Income by States since 1929, Supplement to the Survey of Current Business, 1956.

TABLE 4

REGRESSION EQUATION OF AVERAGE REVENUE PER KWH ON URBAN POPULATION, PER CAPITA INCOME, PROPORTION OF HYDROELECTRIC POWER AND REGULATION, 1912-1937

YEAR	NUMBER OF STATES	CONSTANT TERM	REGRESSION COEFFICIENTS AND THEIR STANDARD ERRORS				R^2	
			Urban Population	Per Capita Income*	Proportion Hydroelectric†	Regulation	Including Regulation	Excluding Regulation
I. All Sales								
1912......	47	.663	-.0291 (.0134)	......	-.552 (.062)	.0028 (.0590)	.654	.654
1922......	47	.730	-.0533 (.0240)	......	-.508 (.081)	-.0708 (.0596)	.546	.531
1932......	42	.380	-.0478 (.0144)	.141 (.090)	-.336 (.058)	-.0630 (.0409)	.580	.554
1937......	39	.323	-.0486 (.0157)	.123 (.121)	-.257 (.059)	-.102 (.043)	.496	.413
II. Sales to Domestic Customers								
1932......	42	1.036	-.0044 (.0125)	-.0804 (.0781)	-.132 (.050)	-.0371 (.0358)	.286	.266
1937......	39	.726	-.0223 (.0130)	.0187 (.1002)	-.146 (.409)	-.0337 (.0358)	.271	.251
III. Sales to Commercial and Industrial Customers								
1932......	42	.622	-.0496 (.0149)	......	-.349 (.059)	-.0306 (.0391)	.546	.539
1937......	39	.572	-.0520 (.0159)	......	-.262 (.061)	-.0925 (.0417)	.493	.422

*Per capita income variable introduced only in years in which annual data are available.

†In 1912 and 1922, ratio of HP capacity of water wheels and turbines to HP capacity of all prime movers; in 1932 and 1937, ratio of HP capacity of hydroelectric to KW capacity of all generators.

TABLE 5

DIFFERENTIALS BY SIZE OF MONTHLY CONSUMPTION
1924 AND 1936

Year	Class of States	Number of States	Average Ratio of Larger to Smaller Monthly Bills
A. 100 and 25 KWH per Month Bills			
1924.....	Regulated	29	3.02
	Unregulated	10	3.25
1936.....	Regulated	30	2.79
	Unregulated	9	2.86
B. 250 and 100 KWH per Month Bills			
1924.....	Regulated	29	1.90
	Unregulated	10	2.15
1936.....	Regulated	30	1.83
	Unregulated	9	1.82

Source: U.S. Federal Power Commission, "Trends in Residential Rates from 1924 to 1936" (Washington, D.C., 1937), table 11. The observations are unweighted average rates for cities of over 50,000 population in each state.

(see table 6). The ratios are therefore directly opposite to those which were expected.[5] But a scatter diagram analysis reveals that the ratio of domestic to industrial rates depends primarily upon the average number of KWH sold to domestic customers divided by the average number of KWH sold to industrial customers, and the relationship does not not differ between regulated and unregulated states.[6] Again no effect of regulation is detectable.

Stockholder Experience

The final area to which we look for effects of regulation is investors' experience. Our basic test is this: did investors in companies which were not regulated, or were regulated for only a few years, do better than investors in companies which were regulated from an early date?

TABLE 6

AVERAGE RATIO OF DOMESTIC TO INDUSTRIAL PRICE PER KWH

	1917	1937
Regulated states.....	1.616 (29 states)	2.459 (32 states)
Unregulated states...	1.445 (16 states)	2.047 (7 states)

To answer this question, we invest $1,000 in each electrical utility in 1907, reinvest all dividends and cash value of rights, and calculate the accumulated investment in 1920.[7] The year 1907 was chosen as the first date to reduce the possible impact of expectations of regulation, and even this date—which is later than we should like—reduced the number of companies we could trace to 20. The basic data are given in table 7.

The pattern of increases in market values appears erratic. A simple regression of market value as a function of the increase in dollar sales of the utility system and the number of years of regulation is presented in table 8. There is thus a slight, statistically insignificant effect of regulation on market values.[8]

TABLE 7

MARKET VALUE IN 1920 OF INVESTMENT OF $1,000 IN 1907
(20 Electric Companies)

Year of Regulation	Company	Market Value in 1920	Relative Change in Sales 1907-20 (Per Cent)
1887	*Massachusetts:*		
	Edison Electric Illuminating Co. of Boston	$1,689	246
	Lowell Electric Light Corporation	1,485	295
	New Bedford Gas & Edison Light Co.	1,528	164
	Edison Electric Illuminating Co. of Brockton	2,310	558
1907	*New York:*		
	Buffalo General Electric Co.	2,632	718
	Kings County Electric Light & Power Co.	2,356	279
	N.Y. and Queens Electric Light & Power Co.	1,059	225
1909	*Michigan:*		
	Detroit Edison Co.	4,273	1,412
	Houghton County Electric Light Co.	1,959	130
1910	*Maryland:*		
	Consolidated Gas, Electric Light & Power Co. (Baltimore)	6,547	286
	New Jersey:		
	Public Service Corp. of New Jersey	1,546	206
1911	*Ohio:*		
	Columbia Gas and Electric Co.	3,952	999
	Connecticut:		
	Hartford Electric Light Co.	2,028	728
	California:		
	Pacific Gas and Electric Co.	2,051	212
1913	*Illinois:*		
	Commonwealth Edison Co.	2,179	299
1914	*Pennsylvania:*		
	Philadelphia Electric Co.	4,254	296
Not regulated in 1920			
	Galveston-Houston Electric Co.	1,001	262
	Northern Texas Electric Co.	4,861	272
	El Paso Electric Co.	4,046	281
	Tampa Electric Co.	2,830	183

TABLE 8

REGRESSION EQUATIONS OF MARKET VALUE IN 1918 AND 1920 OF
$1,000 INVESTMENT IN 1907, ON GROWTH
IN SALES AND REGULATION*

(20 Electric Companies)

Terminal Year (t)	Constant Term	Growth in Sales	Regulation	R^2
1918..........	3.28	.332 (.227)	- .015 (.010)	.16
1920..........	3.27	.395 (.232)	- .017 (.010)	.21

*Market values in logarithms; growth in sales = log
$(sales_t/sales_{1907})$.

CONCLUSION

Our study was undertaken primarily to investigate the feasibility of measuring the effects of regulation, but our inability to find any significant effects of the regulation of electrical utilities calls for some explanation. This finding is contingent upon our criteria of regulation and of the areas in which we sought effects, but both of these criteria are accepted by much of the literature of public utility economics.

The ineffectiveness of regulation lies in two circumstances. The first circumstance is that the individual utility system is not possessed of any large amount of long run monopoly power. It faces the competition of other energy sources in a large proportion of its product's uses, and it faces the competition of other utility systems, to which in the long run its industrial (and hence many of its domestic) users may move. Let the long run demand elasticity of one utility system be on the order of -8; then the system faces demand and marginal revenue curves such as those displayed in figure 2. Given the cost curves we sketch, price will be MP.[9]

The second circumstance is that the regulatory body is incapable of forcing the utility to operate at a specified combination of output, price, and cost. As we have drawn the curves, there is no market price that represents the announced goal of competitve profits; let us assume that the commission would set a price equal to average cost at some output moderately in excess of output OM, say at R. Since accounting costs are hardly unique, there is a real question whether the regulatory body can even distinguish between costs of MS and MP. Let the commission be given this

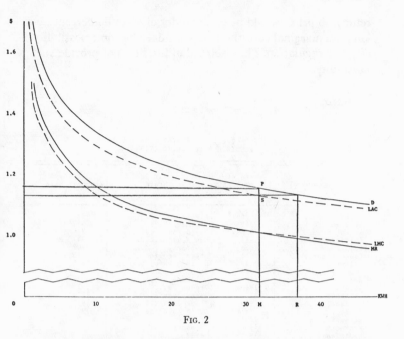

FIG. 2

knowledge; then the utility can reduce costs below *MS* by reducing one or more dimensions of the services which are really part of its output: peak load capacity, constancy of current, promptness of repairs, speed of installation of service. It can also manipulate its average price by suitable changes in the complex rate structure (also with effects on costs). Finally, recognize that the cost curve falls through time, and recognize also the inevitable time lags of a regulatory process, and the possiblity becomes large that the commission will proudly win each battlefield that its protagonist has abandoned except for a squad of lawyers. Since a regulatory body cannot effectively control the daily detail of business operations, it cannot deal with variables whose effects on profits are of the same order of magnitude as the effects of the variables upon which it does have some influence.

The theory of price regulation must, in fact, be based upon the tacit assumption that in its absence a monopoly has exorbitant power. If it were true that pure monopoly profits in the absence of regulation would be 10 or 20 percent above the competitive rate of return, so prices would be on the order of 40 or 80 percent above long run marginal cost, there might indeed be some possibility of effective regulation. The electrical utilities do not provide such a possibility.

APPENDIX

TABLE A1

DATES OF CREATION OF STATE COMMISSION
ELECTRIC RATE JURISDICTION

State	Date of Electric Rate Jurisdiction	State	Date of Electric Rate Jurisdiction
Alabama.............	1915[a,b]	Nevada................	1911
Arizona............	1912	New Hampshire.........	1911[f,c]
Arkansas...........	1935[c,d]	New Jersey............	1910
California.........	1911	New Mexico............	1941[o]
Colorado...........	1913[e]	New York..............	1907[f]
Connecticut........	1911[f,g]	North Carolina........	1913
Delaware...........	1949	North Dakota..........	1919
Florida............	1951	Ohio..................	1911[j]
Georgia............	1907	Oklahoma..............	1913[p]
Idaho..............	1913	Oregon................	1912
Illinois...........	1913	Pennsylvania..........	1914[f]
Indiana............	1913	Rhode Island..........	1912
Iowa...............	[h,i]	South Carolina........	1922[q]
Kansas.............	1911[j]	South Dakota..........	[h]
Kentucky...........	1934	Tennessee.............	1919
Louisiana..........	1934[k]	Texas.................	[h]
Maine..............	1913	Utah..................	1917
Maryland...........	1910	Vermont...............	1908
Massachusetts......	1887[g,l]	Virginia..............	1914[r]
Michigan...........	1909[j]	Washington............	1911
Minnesota..........	[h]	West Virginia.........	1913
Mississippi........	1956	Wisconsin.............	1907
Missouri...........	1913[f,g]	Wyoming...............	1915[g]
Montana............	1913	Washington, D.C.	1913
Nebraska...........	[m,n]		

Source: State laws, statutes, Public Utility Commission reports; Bonbright and Co. and F.P.C. surveys, and correspondence with commission, unless otherwise noted.

[a] No jurisdiction to change existing contracts.

[b] No jurisdiction over contracts with municipalities.

[c] Approves changes in rates only (i.e., new rates).

[d] "Concurrent jurisdiction" with municipalities. Commission hears appeals.

[e] 1921 Court decision: no authority in cities controlling public utilities under home-rule amendment of 1912. Denver (a home-rule city) voted to surrender control to commission in early 1950's. Number of home-rule cities in which commission has no jurisdiction is given as 13 in 1954.

[f] Sets maximum rates only.

[g] Power to investigate upon complaint only.

[h] None through 1960.

[i] Authority outside cities, 1954.

[j] Municipalities fix rates; commission hears appeals only.

[k] Power to fix rates in New Orleans, and other cities voting to surrender control, from 1921 on, subject to optional powers of municipalities. Primary control shifted from municipalities to state commission in 1934.

[l] Source: Barnes, I., "Public Utility Control in Massachusetts," 1930,

p. 96.   Requirement to furnish information to Gas and Electric Commission begins 1908.

[m]None in cities through 1960.

[n]Most companies are public.

[o]Commission had jurisdiction in cities under 10,000 population from 1921 on.

[p]Right to change rates fixed by municipal franchise established by 1915 court decisions.

[q]Jurisdiction over maximum electric rates, on complaint, granted in 1910, but no rate cases reported. In 1922, power of commission extended to allow fixing of rates on own motion. 1922 report indicates jurisdiction over electric utilities considered "recent" by commission.

[r]Excludes services rendered to a municipal corporation in 1914. In 1918, power strengthened so that utilities cannot change rates without commission approval.

(*Appendix continued on next page*)

TABLE A2

AVERAGE REVENUE PER KWH BY STATE, IN CENTS, 1907-37

	1907	1912	1917	1922	1927	1932	1937
Maine.............	1.90	1.42	1.51	1.62	2.06	1.96	2.03
New Hampshire.....	2.36	1.69	1.78	3.92	4.39	3.80	3.03
Vermont...........	2.62	1.91	2.21	1.89	*	*	*
Massachusetts.....	4.66	3.96	2.82	3.23	3.74	3.79	3.05
Rhode Island......	4.50	3.44	2.32	2.32	*	*	*
Connecticut.......	3.50	3.53	2.64	3.25	3.46	3.56	2.81
New York..........	2.19	2.22	1.86	2.09	2.58	3.05	2.21
New Jersey........	4.17	2.71	2.50	3.22	4.04	3.97	3.03
Pennsylvania......	3.49	2.22	1.50	2.15	2.40	2.55	1.96
Ohio..............	3.38	2.75	1.85	2.36	2.60	2.73	2.01
Indiana...........	3.18	2.86	2.42	3.02	2.89	3.11	2.24
Illinois..........	2.94	2.28	1.93	2.24	2.62	2.68	2.20
Michigan..........	2.22	1.89	1.46	2.01	2.40	2.67	1.94
Wisconsin.........	3.67	2.36	1.82	2.43	2.77	3.18	2.41
Minnesota.........	2.74	2.76	1.74	2.85	3.14	3.15	2.63
Iowa..............	5.44	5.23	1.29	1.94	3.72	3.79	2.66
Missouri..........	3.57	3.56	2.86	3.10	2.83	2.64	2.22
North Dakota......	5.69	6.52	7.05	6.73	8.02	6.01	4.36
South Dakota......	3.35	4.03	5.41	5.58	7.27	5.65	4.33
Nebraska..........	4.44	4.41	3.11	3.59	3.57	3.24	2.78
Kansas............	2.20	1.77	2.08	2.68	3.27	3.29	2.66
Virginia..........	3.05	2.40	1.72	1.88	2.44	2.65	2.22
West Virginia.....	2.44	2.32	1.55	1.36	*	*	1.59
North Carolina....	2.70	1.08	1.34	2.12	1.30	1.79	1.59
South Carolina....	1.07	.86	.48	1.01	1.54	1.65	*
Georgia...........	1.23	1.45	1.13	1.27	1.97	2.19	*
Florida...........	5.94	4.91	4.54	5.24	5.51	4.59	3.90
Kentucky..........	4.01	3.65	3.38	3.55	3.20	3.12	2.30
Tennessee.........	3.61	2.78	.70	2.04	2.40	1.90	1.99
Alabama...........	2.92	2.22	.79	1.22	1.66	1.69	*
Mississippi.......	4.08	3.38	3.66	4.66	4.67	3.59	*
Arkansas..........	5.84	5.50	4.01	4.33	4.46	3.22	2.64
Louisiana.........	4.53	3.86	3.27	5.26	3.05	2.55	2.06
Oklahoma..........	4.32	4.37	3.24	3.39	3.26	3.12	2.36
Texas.............	4.82	4.38	2.94	3.18	3.09	2.82	2.36
Montana...........	1.57	.84	.74	.81	*	*	*
Idaho.............	4.85	1.22	1.37	.70	2.00	2.06	1.56
Wyoming...........	5.51	5.08	3.32	4.97	5.17	4.49	3.64
Colorado..........	2.57	2.49	2.09	2.85	3.39	4.10	3.10
New Mexico........	5.66	4.93	4.93	5.32	7.15	*	*
Arizona...........	5.72	3.12	2.65	2.59	2.53	*	*
Utah..............	9.01	1.42	.98	4.41	*	*	*
Nevada............	1.14	1.34	1.46	1.65	2.54	2.70	2.47
Washington........	1.06	2.57	1.66	1.41	1.51	1.45	1.44
Oregon............	1.94	2.09	2.11	1.39	2.09	2.10	1.89
California........	1.97	1.39	1.29	1.57	2.18	2.20	1.82

Source: U.S. Bureau of the Census, Census of Electrical Industries, quinquennial.

* Not presented separately to avoid disclosure of information for individual establishments. Where data for two or more adjoining states are presented, the combined data were used provided the states in the combination had the same regulation status in the year under consideration. Rates for combinations employed are as follows: Vermont and Rhode Island, 1927 = 3.44, 1932 = 3.54, 1937 = 2.81; Montana and Utah, 1927 = 1.08, 1932 = 1.94, 1937 =1.13; Delaware, Maryland, and Washington, D.C., 1907 = 3.68, 1912 = 3.22, 1917 = 2.01, 1922 = 2.52, 1937 = 1.95; Delaware, Maryland, Washington, D.C., and West Virginia, 1927 = 2.39, 1932 = 2.35. Combinations of Delaware with adjoining states do not meet the above criterion but are included because Delaware's rated horsepower capacity is less than 10 per cent (in 1927) of the total for either combination.

AVERAGE REVENUE PER KWH BY STATE AND TYPE
OF CUSTOMER, IN CENTS, 1932 AND 1937

STATE	DOMESTIC		COMMERCIAL AND INDUSTRIAL	
	1932	1937	1932	1937
Maine......................	6.4	5.3	1.4	1.5
New Hampshire............	7.3	5.6	2.9	2.4
Vermont and Rhode Island	7.0*	5.8*	2.7*	2.2*
Massachusetts............	6.1	5.3	3.0	2.4
Connecticut..............	5.5	4.6	2.8	2.3
New York.................	6.2	5.0	2.4	1.8
New Jersey...............	7.3	5.5	3.1	2.4
Pennsylvania.............	5.9	4.6	2.0	1.6
Ohio.....................	5.4	3.9	2.2	1.6
Indiana..................	6.0	4.7	2.5	1.8
Illinois.................	5.3	4.3	2.0	1.8
Michigan.................	4.4	3.5	2.2	1.6
Wisconsin................	5.4	3.8	2.6	2.0
Minnesota................	5.7	4.1	2.6	2.2
Iowa.....................	6.6	5.0	2.8	2.1
Missouri.................	4.9	3.9	2.2	1.8
North Dakota.............	7.0	4.7	5.4	4.2
South Dakota.............	7.1	5.1	4.9	3.9
Nebraska.................	5.7	4.6	2.7	2.3
Kansas...................	5.5	4.9	2.5	2.1
Delaware, Maryland, and Washington, D.C........	†	3.8*	†	1.6*
Delaware, Maryland, Washington, D.C., and West Virginia..............	5.0*	....	1.9*	....
Virginia.................	5.6	4.1	2.0	1.8
West Virginia............	†	4.4	†	1.3
North Carolina...........	5.8	3.8	1.4	1.4
South Carolina...........	5.6	*	1.4	*
Georgia..................	5.4	*	1.8	*
Florida..................	6.7	5.3	3.6	3.2
Kentucky.................	6.2	4.2	2.5	1.9
Tennessee................	6.2	3.4	1.4	1.7
Alabama..................	5.3	*	1.4	*
Mississippi..............	6.6	*	3.0	*
Arkansas.................	7.3	5.7	2.6	2.2
Louisiana................	7.6	5.7	1.9	1.6
Oklahoma.................	6.3	5.3	2.6	1.9
Texas....................	6.2	4.8	2.3	1.9
Montana and Utah.........	4.8*	4.0*	1.6*	.9*
Idaho....................	3.6	3.1	1.7	1.3
Wyoming..................	6.8	6.1	3.8	3.0
Colorado.................	6.1	5.5	3.4	2.5
New Mexico...............	*	*	*	*
Arizona..................	*	*	*	*
Nevada...................	5.0	4.2	2.3	2.1
Washington...............	2.7	2.7	1.3	1.2
Oregon...................	3.2	2.8	1.7	1.6
California...............	4.3	3.8	1.8	1.5

Source: U.S. Bureau of the Census, Census of Electrical
Industries, quinquennial.

*
Not presented separately to avoid disclosure of information for individual establishments. See table A2, footnote,
for criterion for inclusion.

†
See combined data for Delaware, Maryland, Washington,
D.C., and West Virginia.

Public Regulation of
the Securities Market

It is doubtful whether any other type of public regulation of economic activity has been so widely admired as the regulation of the securities markets by the Securities and Exchange Commission. The purpose of this regulation is to increase the portion of truth in the world and to prevent or punish fraud, and who can defend ignorance or fraud? The Commission has led a scandal-free life as federal regulatory bodies go [1964!]. It has been essentially a "technical" body, and has enjoyed the friendship, or at least avoided the enmity, of both political parties.

The Report of the Special Study of the Securities Markets, which was recently released, is itself symptomatic of the privileged atmosphere within which the SEC dwells.[1] This study investigated the adequacy of the controls over the security markets now exercised by the SEC. The study was well endowed: it was directed by an experienced attorney, Milton H. Cohen; it had a professional staff of more than thirty people; and it operated on a schedule that was leisurely by Washington standards. The study was not an instrument of some self-serving group, nor was it even seriously limited by positions taken by the administration. Such a professional, disinterested appraisal would not even be conceivable for agricultural or merchant marine or petroleum policy, or the other major areas of public regulation. Disinterest, good will, and money had all joined to improve the capital markets of America.

The regulation of the securities markets is therefore an appropriately antiseptic area in which to see how public policy is formed. Here we should be able to observe past policy appraised, and new policy defended, on an intellectually respectable level, if ever it is.

We begin with an examination of certain of the *Special Study's* policy proposals. Cohen presents a vast number of recommenda-

Reprinted from the *Journal of Business of the University of Chicago* 37, no. 2 (April 1964).

tions of changes in institutions and practices. Most are minor, and some are even frivolous (market letters should not predict specific price levels of stocks). The content of the proposals, however, is not our present concern; what is our concern is the manner in which the proposals are reached. More specifically: (1) How does the Cohen Report show that an existing practice or institution is defective? (2) How does the Cohen Report show that the changes it recommends (*a*) will improve the situation, and (*b*) are better in some sense than alternative proposals? In answering these questions I shall use the discussion of the qualifications of brokers and other personnel in the industry (chap. 2), although the numerous other areas would do quite as well.

THE FORMULATION OF POLICY

The Cohen Report tells us that there is cause for dissatisfaction with the personnel of the industry: "From the evidence gathered by the study, it appears that the existing controls have proven to be deficient in some important regards. The dishonest broker-dealer, that 'greatest menace to the public,' to use the words of one Commission official, continues to appear with *unjustifiable frequency*. Also, the inexperienced broker-dealer *too often* blunders into problems for himself, his customers, and the regulatory agencies" (chap. 2, p. 51; my italics). So there are too many thieves and too many incompetents.

How does Cohen prove that there are enough thieves and incompetents to justify more stringent controls? After all, one can always find some dishonest and untutored men in a group of 100,000: not all the angels in heaven have good posture.

The "proof" of the need for further regulatory measures consists basically and almost exclusively of four case studies. These studies briefly describe four new firms with relatively inexperienced salesmen who were caught in falling markets and in three cases became bankrupt or withdrew from the business. No estimates of losses to customers are made. The studies were handpicked to emphasize the shortcomings of *new* firms, because this is the place where Cohen wishes to impose new controls. The studies are of course worthless as a proof of the need for new policies: nothing Cohen, the SEC, or the United States government can do will make it difficult to find four more cases at any time one looks for them.

Cohen's second, and only other, piece of evidence, is a survey of disciplinary actions against members of the NASD (National Association of Security Dealers) from 1959 through 1961. To quote the report: "The results of this analysis revealed that the association's newest member firms, which are generally controlled by persons having less experience than principals of older firms, were responsible for a heavy preponderance of the offenses drawing the most severe penalties" (part 1, p. 66). Cohen's summary of the statistical study, of which this sentence is a fair sample, would not meet academic standards of accuracy. The study reveals that of 1,014 firms founded before 1941, 223 were involved in disciplinary proceedings between 1959 and 1961; of 1,072 firms founded in 1959–60, only 103 were involved in such proceedings. The data are poorly tabulated (dismissals are included, and duplicate charges against one firm are counted as several firms), but however viewed they do not make a case for the need for more regulation, or for more severe screening of new entrants.[2] Yet Cohen believes that the basis has been laid for his main finding:

> The large number of new investors and new broker-dealer firms and salesmen attracted to the securities industry in recent years have combined to create a problem of major dimensions. . . .
>
> More than a generation of experience with the Federal securities laws has demonstrated, moreover, that it is impossible to regulate effectively the conduct of those in the securities industry, unless would-be members are adequately screened at the point of entry [part 1, p. 150].

These alleged findings lead to a series of policy proposals, such as the following:

1. All brokers should be compelled to join "self-regulatory" agencies (such as the NASD).

2. No one who has been convicted of embezzlement, fraud, or theft should be allowed in the industry for ten years thereafter.

3. A good character should be required for entrants.

4. Examinations should be required for prospective entrants.

The *Report* approves strongly of the six-month training period now required of customers' men in firms belonging to the New York Stock Exchange (NYSE).

Cohen believes that the people dealing in securities with the public should have extensive training and screening such as his own profession requires. My lengthy experience with "account executives" of major NYSE firms has not uncovered knowledge beyond what would fit comfortably into a six-hour course. It would have been most useful if Cohen had investigated the experience of customers of a randomly chosen set of account men with diverse amounts of training and experience: Have differences in experience or training had any effect on the profits of their customers? But he never even dreamed of the possibility—or perhaps it was of the need—of pretesting his proposals.

The report takes for granted not only the effectiveness but also, what is truly remarkable, the infallibility of the regulating process:

> There is no evidence that these practices are typical . . .
> but regardless of their frequency they represent problems too important to be ignored [part 1, p. 268].
> The mere fact that there have been any losses at all is sufficient reason to consider whether there are further adjustments that should be made for the protection of investors [part 1, p. 400].

Observe: no matter how infrequent or trivial the damage to investors, the regulatory process must seek to eliminate it (no doubt inexpensively). Surely rhetoric has replaced reason at this point.

As for alternative methods of dealing with the problem of fraud, only one is mentioned: "A number of persons have suggested that a Federal fidelity or surety bond requirement be imposed in addition to or in lieu of a capital requirement. It would seem, however, that such a requirement would present a number of practical difficulties and that more significant protection to the public can be assured through a Federal net capital requirement. No recommendation as to bonding, therefore, will be made at this time" (part 1, p. 92). I must confess to being shocked by this passage. A number of "practical difficulties" exclude the sensible, direct, efficient way to deal with the problem of financial responsibility—difficulties so obvious and conclusive they do not even need to be mentioned.

When one looks at a well-built theater set from the angle at which the audience is to view it, it appears solid and convincing. When one looks from another direction, it is a set of two-dimensional pieces of cardboard and canvas, which could not possibly create an illusion of validity. So it is with the Cohen Report. Once we ask for the evidence for its policy proposals, the immense enterprise becomes a promiscuous collection of conventional beliefs and personal prejudices.

A TEST OF PREVIOUS REGULATION

A proposal of public policy, everyone should agree, is open to criticism if it omits a showing that the proposal will serve its announced goal. Yet the proposal may be a desirable and opportune one, and the inadequacies of a proposer are no proof of the undesirability of the proposal. And—to leave the terrain of abstract and unctuous truth—the past work of the SEC and Cohen's schemes for its future may serve fine purposes even though no statistician has measured these probable achievements. Quite so. But then again, perhaps not.

The paramount goal of the regulations in the security markets is to protect the innocent (but avaricious) investor. A partial test of the effects of the SEC on investors' fortunes will help to answer the question of whether testing a policy's effectiveness is an academic scruple or a genuine need. This partial test will serve also to illustrate the kind of study that should have occupied the *Special Study.*[3]

The basic test is simplicity itself: how did investors fare before and after the SEC was given control over the registration of new issues? We take all the new issues of industrial stocks with a value exceeding $2.5 million in 1923–27, and exceeding $5 million in 1949–55, and measure the values of these issues (compared to their offering price) in five subsequent years. It is obviously improper to credit or blame the SEC for the absolute differences between the two periods in investors' fortunes, but if we measure stock prices relative to the market average, we shall have eliminated most of the effects of general market conditions. The price ratios (p_t/p_0) for each time span are divided by the ratio of the market average for the same period. Thus if from 1924 to 1926 a common stock rose from $20 to $30, the price ratio is 150 (percent) or an increase of 50 percent but, relative to the market, which rose by 47.0 percent over this two-year period, the new issue rose only 2 percent.

The choice of the time periods over which to judge the performance of the SEC review is intuitive: *immediately* after a new issue is floated, its price has not changed enough as a rule to reveal the outcome of purchase; *long after* the flotation the price is dominated by events which took place after the purchase. Clearly this intuitive argument, though plausible, gives no explicit guidance: the right period to study could be six months or six years.

At any date after the individual purchases a new issue, he has three types of information on which to act: (1) the information available through private channels at the time of flotation, which would include information on the industry as well as on the firm; (2) the information provided only because it is demanded by SEC requirements; (3) information which appears subsequent to the flotation. In practice the distinction between types (1) and (2) would often be hard to draw: the SEC supporter will claim all the improvements over time in type (1) information are due to his agency; the more detached scholar will study the improvements in information which came before 1934, and in areas not subject to regulation. If the distinction is feasible, we could make a direct test of the SEC registration procedure by analyzing stock prices to determine the influence of the SEC-dictated information.[4] In fact, unless such tests can be made, there is no objective way of deciding which kinds and amounts of information to require in a registration statement.

To return to our problem of the period of possible effect of the disclosures in the registration statement, I believe that the effective time intervals should be approximately one to two years. Consider the purchase of the stock of a new company: its preflotation history will be brief and meager, and the prospects at flotation time will be completely submerged by the results of the next two years of operation. Or consider an established enterprise: its preflotation history is lengthy and substantial, so the disclosures in the prospectus must report chiefly very recent changes, which again are confirmed or refuted by the events of the next year or two.

The annual averages of the quotations (relative to market) are given for common stocks in table 1. In both periods it was an unwise man who bought new issues of common stock: he lost about one-tenth of his investment in the first year relative to the market, and another tenth in the years that followed. The data reveal no risk aversion.

TABLE 1

COMMON STOCKS. INDEXES OF NEW STOCK PRICES
RELATIVE TO MARKET AVERAGES

(Issue Year = 100)

PERIOD	YEAR AFTER ISSUE				
	1	2	3	4	5
Pre-SEC:					
1923............	90.4	81.5	76.4	63.7	73.6
1924............	104.1	81.8	77.2	74.5	59.7
1925............	87.2	72.6	61.1	51.2	43.3
1926............	88.4	83.2	84.8	64.8	67.2
1927............	89.7	76.4	72.7	91.6	127.9
1923-27 average...	89.9	77.9	72.5	66.2	70.7
Standard deviation.....	38.8	45.6	44.4	56.3	80.6
Number of issues	44	46	47	47	47
Post-SEC:					
1949............	92.6	92.1	90.8	90.1	70.4
1950............	102.8	90.6	61.3	68.3	60.9
1951............	89.9	83.9	83.0	86.7	79.8
1952............	91.6	75.9	72.9	72.2	73.2
1953............	91.1	86.6	86.5	81.1	86.7
1954............	67.8	61.9	69.0	55.5	51.8
1955............	74.5	68.9	89.6	87.2	94.2
1949-55 average...	87.9	79.1	78.4	77.7	74.9
Standard deviation.....	21.2	25.1	27.7	27.6	36.0
Number of issues	46	46	46	46	46

[Source: see appendix to tables at end of this chapter.]

The averages for the two periods reveal no difference in values after one or two years, but a significant difference in the third and fourth, but not fifth, years.

These comparisons suggest that the investors in common stocks in the 1950s did little better than in the 1920s, indeed clearly no better if they held the securities only one or two years. In fact the differences between the averages in the two periods are not statistically significant in any year. This comparison is incomplete in that dividends are omitted from our reckoning, although this is probably a minor omission and may well work in favor of the 1920s.[5]

The variance of the price ratios, however, was much larger in the 1920s than in the later period: in every year the difference between periods was significant at the 1 percent level, and in four years at the 0.1 percent level. This is a most puzzling finding: the simple-minded interpretation is that the SEC has succeeded in eliminating both unusually good and unusually bad new issues! This is difficult to believe as a matter of either intent or accident. A more plausible explanation lies in the fact that many more new companies used the market in the 1920s than in the 1950s—from one viewpoint a major effect of the SEC was to exclude new companies.[6]

An interesting characteristic of the security prices is their correlation at various dates. If the correlation between issue price and price t years later rose from the pre- to the post-SEC period, as compared with the correlation between prices at p_k and p_{k+t} (a later interval of equal length), one would be inclined to credit the SEC's requirements with having improved the structure of issue prices (as judged by subsequent developments). There was in fact such a change in the correlation coefficients, and an improvement in the structure of issue prices may be due to the SEC.[7]

The preferred stocks, which were far more numerous than the common stocks in the 1920s, pose a special problem. We use the market average as the base for measuring investor experience in order to minimize the influence of other factors, but no such market average exists for preferred stocks. The existing preferred stock indexes are actually indexes of the yields of preferred stocks, and exclude defaults or failures, so they do not measure the fortunes of investors in preferred stocks.

The price relatives for preferred stocks are compared with both issue price and common-stock indexes in table 2. Neither base is ideal. I have constructed as a *pis aller* an index of preferred stocks which combines the above-average price relatives based upon issue price and the Standard and Poor Index in the proportions of inconvertible to convertible issues (roughly, 2 to 1 in the 1920s; 1

TABLE 2

PREFERED STOCKS, INDEXES OF NEW STOCK PRICES RELATIVE TO ISSUE YEAR AND RELATIVE TO MARKET AVERAGES

(Issue Year = 100)

A. NEW STOCK PRICES RELATIVE TO ISSUE YEAR--PREFERRED STOCKS

PERIOD	YEAR AFTER ISSUE				
	1	2	3	4	5
Pre-SEC:					
1923..........	95.5	96.5	92.7	97.7	94.6
1924..........	86.4	73.1	68.7	68.7	49.9
1925..........	104.7	103.8	106.4	104.3	79.0
1926..........	100.1	97.3	94.0	86.4	62.8
1927..........	102.5	99.2	92.4	62.1	43.1
1923-27 average..	100.1	97.6	94.9	85.2	65.4
Standard deviation.....	17.0	30.7	36.9	53.5	55.2
Number of issues	63	69	72	68	65
Post-SEC:					
1949..........	112.3	101.7	101.1	97.7	105.2
1950..........	101.3	97.1	96.4	104.6	106.3
1951..........	101.1	94.3	101.8	108.8	113.1
1952..........	95.7	93.6	113.2	95.0	91.2
1953..........	148.1	117.6	119.5	104.5	n.a.
1954..........	112.1	102.7	88.5	77.3	88.3
1955..........	103.6	102.0	109.2	190.5	205.7
1949-55 average..	107.2	99.0	101.9	107.8	114.4
Standard deviation.....	18.5	13.7	20.3	51.9	66.5
Number of issues	40	38	36	33	29

TABLE 2--Continued

B. NEW STOCK PRICES RELATIVE TO MARKET AVERAGES--PREFERRED STOCKS

PERIOD	YEAR AFTER ISSUE				
	1	2	3	4	5
Pre-SEC:					
1923..........	91.4	72.6	60.4	50.8	36.6
1924..........	67.9	49.7	37.6	27.7	16.0
1925..........	90.6	72.0	54.7	42.5	41.8
1926..........	80.2	57.8	57.3	44.2	52.8
1927..........	75.9	58.2	70.5	74.0	100.4
1923-27 average..	82.3	63.2	56.5	53.5	59.6
Standard deviation.....	15.1	19.9	25.2	40.0	74.5
Number of issues	63	69	72	68	65
Post-SEC:					
1949..........	91.9	67.2	61.2	59.0	52.2
1950..........	81.1	71.8	62.1	63.4	46.0
1951..........	92.5	86.1	76.3	58.2	51.5
1952..........	95.6	76.7	66.3	47.3	47.4
1953..........	121.6	68.9	59.6	54.5	n.a.
1954..........	79.9	62.4	56.2	47.4	43.5
1955..........	88.2	90.8	93.8	131.4	146.8
1949-55 average..	91.5	76.9	69.5	62.2	59.1
Standard deviation.....	15.1	14.0	16.7	37.2	49.3
Number of issues	40	38	36	33	29

[Source: see appendix to tables at end of this chapter.]

to 2 in the 1950s). On this compromise basis, the average preferred-stock prices do not differ significantly in the two periods, as is shown in table 3. The preferred-stock data deserve less weight than the common-stock data until a suitable preferred-stock index is developed. Meanwhile the best estimate is that the preferred stocks support the same conclusion as the common stocks.

TABLE 3

WEIGHTED AVERAGE PREFERRED STOCK PRICES RELATIVES
(Issue Year = 100)

PERIOD	YEARS AFTER ISSUE				
	1	2	3	4	5
1923-27.....	94.2	86.1	82.1	74.6	63.5
1949-55.....	96.7	84.3	80.3	77.4	77.5

[Source: see appendix to tables at end of this chapter.]

These studies suggest that the SEC registration requirements had no important effect on the quality of new securities sold to the public. A fuller statistical study—extending to lower sizes of issues and dividend records—should serve to confirm or qualify this conclusion, but it is improbable that the qualification will be large, simply because the issues here included account for most of the dollar volume of industrial stocks issued in these periods. Our study is not exhaustive in another sense: we could investigate the changing industrial composition of new issues and other possible sources of differences in the market performance of new issues in the two periods.

But these admissions of the possibility of closer analysis can be made after any empirical study. They do not affect our two main conclusions: (1) it is possible to study the effects of public policies, and not merely to assume that they exist and are beneficial, and (2) grave doubts exist whether if account is taken of costs of regulation,[8] the SEC has saved the purchasers of new issues one dollar.

THE CRITERIA OF
MARKET EFFICIENCY

So far as the efficiency and growth of the American economy are concerned, efficient capital markets are even more important than the protection of investors—in fact efficient capital markets *are* the major protection of investors. The *Special Study* devotes considerable attention to the mechanism of the most important single market, the New York Stock Exchange.

One can ask whether this market is competitively organized: are the prices of brokers' services set by competitive forces? The answer is clearly in the negative and the Cohen Report is properly critical of the structure of commissions of the NYSE, which is highly discriminatory against higher-priced stocks and larger transactions. The *Report* explicitly refrains from discussing the compulsory minimum rates set by this self-regulating cartel. The reason for silence is obscure: the present scheme of compulsory private price-fixing of brokers' services seems to me wholly objectionable. The replacement of cartel pricing by competition, with review lodged in the Antitrust Division, would confer larger benefits upon investors than the SEC has yet provided.

The mechanism of response to changing conditions is a more subtle matter, dealt with especially in chapter 6 ("Exchange Markets") of the *Special Study*. The task of providing continuity and orderliness of markets in specific stocks is now performed by the specialists, aided or observed (as the case may be) by the floor traders. How well do they presently perform their tasks?

1. The NYSE uses a "tick test" of the effects of specialists on short-run price fluctuations. If a transaction takes place below the last different price, it is called a minus tick, and if above the last different price, it is a plus tick. Purchases on minus ticks and sales on plus ticks are considered stabilizing, and in three sample weeks, 83.9 percent of specialists' transactions were of this type. The *Special Study* rejects this test on two grounds:

> 1. "A tick by itself does not necessarily represent a change in the public's evaluation of the security." Thus, after a transaction at 35, the specialists will often offer 34½ and ask 35½, and a transaction at either price is a so-called stabilizing tick. This represents "only a random sequence of buy and sell orders."

2. The specialists' own profit incentive is to buy low and sell high—and presumably (but the *Special Study* does not say explicitly) no virtue attaches to profitable activity. (*Special Study*, part 2, pp. 102-3)

The *Special Study* demands that the test be applied to a longer sequence of transactions; on individual pairs of transactions the test "can be expected to reveal only cases of grossly destabilizing activity" (ibid., p. 104). Specialists engage in only a third of all transactions, but as a rule at least one-third of the ticks in a stock are negative and one-third positive in a day. Hence the specialists could foster market movements while appearing to stabilize them, or so the Report argues. Thus if the specialist sells in the underlined transactions in the following sequence:

$$35 \quad 34 \quad \underline{34\tfrac{3}{4}} \quad 34 \quad \underline{34\tfrac{1}{2}} \quad 33\tfrac{3}{4} \quad \underline{34},$$

he is stabilizing by the tick test while riding with a market trend. This prescient behavior is not documented, nor is a specific tick test proposed.

2. The preferred test of the specialist's effect is how his inventory of stock varies as the market price fluctuates: "That is, a member trading pattern which tends to produce purchase balances on declining stock days and sales balances on rising stock days would indicate that members exert a stabilizing influence on the stock days in which they traded" (part 2, p. 55). An analysis is made of changes in specialists' stock inventories on four days. In each case inventories moved with the market—that is, they were destabilizing. But if the analysis is performed on stocks classified as rising or falling, balances moved in a stabilizing fashion in seven of the eight cases (part 2, p. 108). But *within* these eight groups there were a substantial number of cases in which inventories of stocks moved with the market, so specialist performance left something to be desired. Cohen's standards have not flagged: he expects every specialist to do, not his best, but perfectly.[9]

The economist will have observed that the *Report* has no theory of markets from which valid criteria can be deduced by which to judge experience. The tick test and the "offsetting balances" tests are both lacking of any logical basis: these tests assume that smoothness of price movement is the sign of an efficient market, and it is not. Let us sketch the problem of an efficient market.

The basic function a market serves is to bring buyers and sellers together. If there were a large number of people who sent their bid and ask prices to a single point (market), we should in effect observe the supply and demand functions of elementary economic theory. *The* price that cleared this market would be established—it would be a unique price if there were sufficient traders to produce continuity of supply and demand functions—and trading would stop.

This once-for-all, or at most once-per-period, market differs from most real markets in which new potential buyers and sellers are appearing more or less irregularly over time. Existing holders of a stock wish to sell it—at a price—to build a home, marry off a daughter, or buy another security which has (for them) greater promise. Existing holders of cash wish to buy the stock, at a price. Neither group is fully identified until after the event: I would become a bidder for a stock that does not fall within my present investment horizon provided that its price falls for reasons which I believe are mistaken.

So demand and supply are flows, and erratic flows with sequences of bids and asks dependent upon the random circumstances of individual traders. As a first approximation, one would expect the number of holders of a security to be proportional to the total value of the issue. Then the numbers of bids, offers, and transactions would also be proportional to the dollar size of the issue. This is roughly true: the turnover rate of a random sample of one hundred stocks in one month is classified by the total value of the issues, in table 4, and only in very small and very large issues was there considerable departure from proportionality.[10]

TABLE 4

TURNOVER RATES OF 100 STOCKS ON THE NEW YORK STOCK
EXCHANGE, MARCH 1961

Value of Issue (Millions of Dollars)	No. of Stocks	Ratio of Shares Traded to Total Outstanding
Under 5...............	9	0.012
5-10.................	12	.026
10-25................	18	.037
25-50................	10	.043
50-75................	11	.073
75-100...............	12	.034
100-250..............	13	.027
250-500..............	8	.029
500 and over.........	7	0.008

Let us take a very primitive model of a random sequence of bids and asks, and see what this sequence implies for (1) the level of transaction prices, and (2) the time until a bid or ask is met and a transaction occurs. We start with a demand schedule (table 5) for a given stock of which 710,000 shares are outstanding, so the equilibrium price is between 29¾ and 30. A sequence of bids and asks now appears. They are truly random: two-digit numbers from a table of random numbers are drawn, and the first digit determines whether it is a bid or ask (even or odd, respectively) and the second digit determines the level of the bid or ask (0–9, or, in market price units, 28¾–31). (This uniform distribution is replaced by a normal distribution later, but it suffices for the present.) The sequence of random numbers (here called "tenders") proceeds:

> (1) 28: a bid (2 is even) of 8 (= 30¾),
> (2) 30: an ask (3 is odd) of 0 (= 29¾),

Here a transaction occurs at 30¾ because this highest outstanding bid exceeds the seller's minimum ask. To proceed:

> (3) 95: an ask of 5,
> (4) 01: a bid of 1,
> (5) 10: an ask of 0.

TABLE 5

DEMAND SCHEDULE FOR
A SECURITY

Price	Aggregate Demand
28¾ (0)..........	800,000
29 (1)..........	780,000
29¼ (2)..........	760,000
29½ (3)..........	740,000
29¾ (4)..........	720,000
30 (5)..........	700,000
30¼ (6)..........	680,000
30½ (7)..........	660,000
30¾ (8)..........	640,000
31 (9)..........	620,000

This last trader sells at 1 (= 29) to the fourth tender. The process continues, with the further rule that any unfulfilled bids or asks are cancelled after twenty-five numbers. The transaction price and the minimum unfulfilled asking price and maximum unfulfilled bid are shown in figure 1.

The transaction prices fluctuate substantially, as will be seen—indeed the mean absolute deviation from the equilibrium price

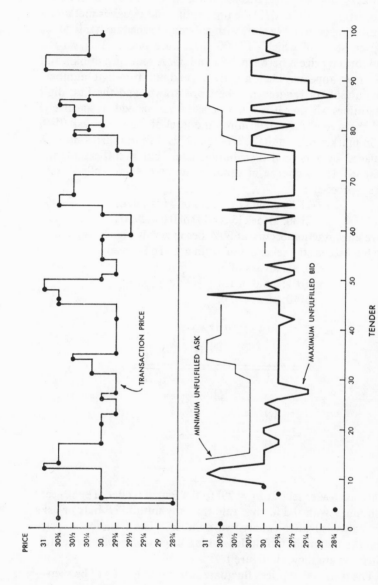

PRICE

31
30¾
30½
30¼
30
29¾
29½
29¼
29
28¾

TRANSACTION PRICE

31
30¾
30½
30¼
30
29¾
29½
29¼
29
28¾

MINIMUM UNFULFILLED ASK

MAXIMUM UNFULFILLED BID

TENDER

FIG. 1.—Hypothetical sequence of transaction prices, generated by sequence of random numbers, and maximum unfulfilled bid and minimum unfulfilled ask prices (equilibrium price of $29\frac{3}{4}$ or 30).

(taken as the closer of 29¾ or 30) is $0.34, or 34 percent of the maximum possible absolute deviation. The average delay in fulfilling a bid or ask is 3.8 units (of tenders).[11] These particular results depend upon the special distribution of bids and asks we assume, but any reasonable distribution will generate significant fluctuations in price and significant and erratic delays in filling bids or asks.

The time unit involved in the foregoing analysis is the interval between successive bids or asks. If tenders are proportional to transactions, and the latter to dollar size of issue, this time unit will be inversely proportional to the size of issue. The time unit will be roughly 1/1,000 as long for American Telephone and Telegraph as for Oklahoma Gas and Electric common. In addition the effective price unit for trading may be ¼ or ½ dollar for the less active stock where it is ⅛ for the active stock.

In addition to allowing buyers and sellers to deal with one another, an efficient market is commonly expected to display the property of resilience (to use an unfamiliar word for a property whose absence is called "thinness"). Resilience is the ability to absorb *market* bid or ask orders (i.e., without a price limit) without an appreciable fluctuation in price. No market can absorb vast orders without large price changes, so this condition must be interpreted as follows: market buy and sell orders of a magnitude consistent with random fluctuation in tenders with an unchanging equilibrium price should not change the transaction prices appreciably.

The reason for making resilience a property of efficient markets may be approached through an analogy. If in a geographical area prices of a product differ, in response to random demand changes, by more than transportation costs, we say that the allocation of the product will be inefficient: A will buy the good for $6 when B is unable to obtain it for $7 (including transportation costs). Alternatively, the owners of the good are not maximizing its value.

Similarly, if random fluctuations in price—under our assumed condition of a stable equilibrium price—lead to price changes greater than inventory carrying costs (the cost of transporting a security from one date to another), the allocation of the product will be inefficient among buyers. Alternatively, the sellers are not maximizing the value of their holdings.

If access to the market is free, speculators will appear to provide resilience by carrying inventories of the stock; they are in fact primarily the specialists of the NYSE plus the floor traders. The speculators will charge the cost of carrying inventories and of their personal services by the bid-ask spread they establish, and in competitive equilibrium this spread will be just remunerative of these trading costs. The technical efficiency with which this inventory management is conducted will be measured by the spread between bid and ask prices.

In addition there are costs of the provision of the machinery of exchange, and these are also part of the cost of transactions. The performance of the main function of the exchange as a market place is subject to economies of scale. The greater the number of transactions in a security concentrated in one exchange, the smaller the discontinuities in trading and the smaller the necessary inventories of securities. As a result the price of a security will almost invariably be "made" in one exchange.

Specialists would then alter the price pattern of figure 1 by setting fixed bid and ask prices (under the present assumption of fixed supply and demand conditions). They will offer to buy all shares at, say, 29¾ and sell to all buyers at 30, and the difference (the "jobber's turn") will be the compensation for the costs of acting as a specialist.[12]

To summarize: the efficient market under stationary conditions of supply and demand has the properties:

1. If a bid equals or exceeds the lowest asking price (and similarly for offers), a transaction takes place

2. Higher bids are fulfilled before lower bids, and conversely for offers

3. Prices will fluctuate only within the limits of speculator's costs of providing a market (under competition).

In this regime the cost of transactions (half the bid-ask spread plus commissions) will be the complete inverse measure of the efficiency of the markets. Bid and ask prices will be (almost) constant through time.[13]

Let us consider now the formidable task of real markets, in which the equilibrium price changes without precise or advance notice. We illustrate the characteristic price patterns in the absence of speculation with figures 2 and 3. The sequences of

bids, asks, and transaction prices follow the procedure of figure 1
with four changes:

1. The random numbers are normally distributed (with $=$ $1.00)

2. In figure 2 the equilibrium price is dropped from $25.00 to
$23.75 after 50 tenders

3. In figure 3 the equilibrium price begins a linear upward trend
of 5 cents per tender after 25 tenders

4. No tenders are cancelled because of staleness.

In each case, after the equilibrium changes the unfulfilled tenders
are alternatively (1) retained, and (2) changed by the amount of
the change in the equilibrium price—the two alternatives bracket
the most reasonable assumptions. If the reader will compare the
equilibrium prices with the observed sequences he will better
appreciate the task of the specialist in detecting true changes and
avoiding false changes in the equilibrium price ($=$ population
value).

If the impacts on equilibrium are sudden and unexpected—as
in the examples underlying figure 2—the appropriate market
response is an immediate and complete shift to the new price
level. Under this condition the demand for "continuity" in a
market is a demand for delay in responding to the change in
demand conditions, and, the *Special Study* to the contrary, there
simply is no merit in such delay.

The popular NYSE practice of suspending trading until buy
and sell orders can be matched at a "reasonable" price is open to
serious objection. To prevent a trade is no function of the
exchange, and any defense must lie in a desire to avoid "unnecessary" price fluctuations. An unnecessary price fluctuation is
surely one not called for by the conditions of supply and demand
of the *week* even though the fluctuation may reflect supply and
demand of the *hour*. This suspension of trading means that the
exchange officials know the correct price change when there is a
flood of buy or sell orders. We need not pause to inquire where
they get this clairvoyance; it is enough to notice that the correct
way to iron out the unnecessary wrinkles in the price chart is to
speculate: to buy or sell against the unnecessary movement. The
omniscient officials should be deprived of the power to suspend
trading but given vast sums to speculate. Since omniscience can

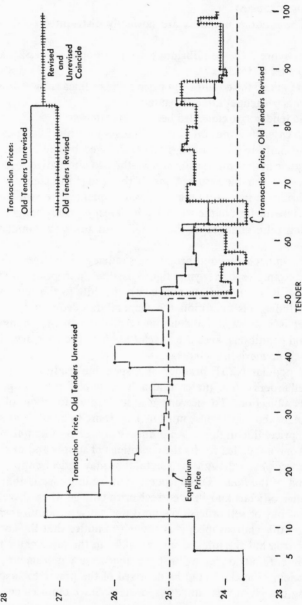

Fig. 2.—Sequence of transaction prices generated by random normal deviates: Equilibrium price of $25.00 for first 50 tenders; equilibrium price of $23.75 thereafter.

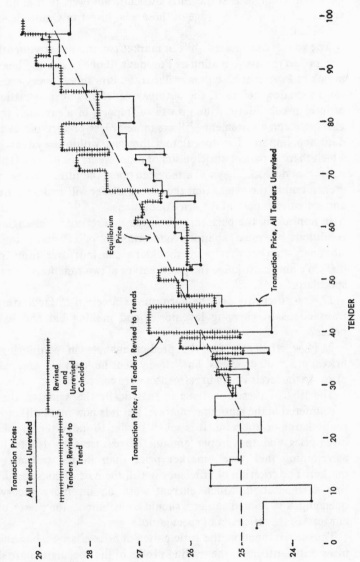

PRICE

29 —

28 —

27 —

26 —

25 —

24—

0   10   20   30   40   50   60   70   80   90   100

TENDER

Transaction Prices:

All Tenders Unrevised

Revised
and
Unrevised
Coincide

Tenders Revised to Trend

Transaction Price, All Tenders Revised to Trends

Transaction Price, All Tenders Unrevised

Equilibrium Price

FIG. 3.—Sequence of transaction prices generated by random normal deviates: Equilibrium price of $25.00 for first 25 tenders increasing by $0.05 per tender thereafter.

surely earn 20 or 50 percent a year on the market, there should be no trouble in raising the capital. To disassociate random from persistent changes is sufficiently difficult, however, to make me very admiring of the courage of those who invest in Omniscience Unlimited.

The wholly unexpected shift in market conditions infrequently occurs—as the assassination of President Kennedy and the heart attack of President Eisenhower illustrate. But almost every event casts a shadow before it: the outbreak of war, the expropriation of foreign subsidiaries, the growth of imports of a product, the glowing income statement—all are more or less predictable as to date and import. The speculators then act within a system in which there is partial anticipation of most events that occur (and many that do not). They will attempt to guess the future course of events, and to the extent that they succeed they will make profits and smooth the path of the price quotations.

In appraising the performance of the market under changing conditions we must abandon our criterion of efficiency in a stationary market that price should be constant over time (p. 000). We now must judge the performance of two functions by the speculator:

1. How efficiently does he perform his function of facilitating transactions by carrying inventories and making bid and ask prices?

2. How efficiently does he predict changes in equilibrium prices, or, in other words, how closely does he keep bid and ask prices to the levels which in retrospect were correct?

The first of these functions is analytically the same as that encountered in the stationary market, but it is now more difficult to discharge or appraise. It is much harder to judge the proper inventories and the proper amount of resources to devote to ascertaining the "true" market price than in the stationary market. The criterion of efficiency is still the cost of consummating a transaction. Much current work on inventory theory, queueing, and related subjects should contribute to the power of our tests of the efficiency of speculators.

The second function, the anticipation of price changes, has one measurable attribute: the trading profits of the speculators are a measure of their skill in anticipating price movements. What is more interesting is that the positive profits of the speculators also demonstrate that their activity stabilizes prices in the sense of reducing the variance of prices over time.[14]

These profits as reported by the *Special Study* have been quite attractive: on liquid capital of $76.3 million in 1960, specialists made a trading income of $21.2 million (part 2, pp. 371, 373), as well as making $19.6 million in commissions. No profitability data are given for floor traders.

CONCLUSION

I have argued at suitable length that the Cohen Report makes poor use of either empirical evidence or economic theory, so its criticisms are founded upon prejudice and its reforms are directed by wishfulness. Full disclosure is the rule of the hour, so I must add that the adacemic scholars have not given the capital markets the attention they deserve because of their importance and analytical fascination. The area is replete with problems in the economics of information: what over-the-counter transactions should be required to be reported? Should floor traders' orders be delayed in execution to achieve parity with outsiders? and the like. It is an equally attractive area for the theory of decisions under uncertainty: what are the ex post criteria of efficient speculation? The prospectuses of research are glowing—should we start censoring this form of literature too?

APPENDIX TO TABLES 1, 2, AND 3

The lists of new flotation of common and preferred stocks are taken from the *Commercial and Financial Chronicle* for the earlier period, and *Investment Dealer's Digest* for the later period. Issues first offered only to stockholders and privately placed issues are excluded, as are public utilities and railroads.

The price quotations are the initial asking price and, at subsequent twelve-month intervals, the averages of the weekly high and low for the week nearest the middle of the month. Averages of monthly highs and lows are employed where weekly quotations are not available. Stock splits and dividends are eliminated, that is, the price of a share is multiplied by the number of shares the original share has become. If an issue of preferred stock is retired, its retirement value is used in the year of retirement, after which it is dropped from the sample.

The price relatives presented here are relative to issue price.

The market index is *Standard and Poor's Annual Industrial Index*. It is said to be biased upward in the early period but not in the later period; this bias would of course exaggerate the influence of the SEC in our tests. *Standard and Poor's Index* covers only common stocks. Tables 1 and 2 of the text summarize information for these price relatives deflated by the relative value of the market index for the same period.

FOUR

Old and New Economic Theories of Regulation

7 The Economists' Traditional Theory of the Economic Functions of the State

Economists have long had a deeply schizophrenic view of the state. They study an elaborate and remarkably complex private economy, and find that by precise and elegant criteria of optimal behavior a private enterprise system has certain classes of failures. These failures, of which some are highly complex in nature and all are uncertain in magnitude, are proposed for remedial or surrogate performance by the state.

Simultaneously, the economists—along with the rest of the population—view the democratic state as a well-meaning, clumsy institution all too frequently diverted by emotion and administered by venality. The state is often viewed as the bulwark of "vested interests"—and in fact where else can an interest vest? The state is thus at one and the same time the corrector of subtle disharmonies between the marginal social and the marginal private products of resources and the obstinately unlearning patron of indefensible protective import quotas and usury laws.

I propose to reexamine both of these positions, and it comes as no surprise to anyone that an economist seldom reexamines traditional views in order to endorse them strongly. In truth I consider both the complex theory of welfare economics—for that is what we call the economic analysis of market failures—and that blend of hope and cynicism which passes for political wisdom to have been infertile and obfuscatory. Let us, then, reexamine the economic theory of the functions of the state.

By the end of the nineteenth century, economists had developed a sophisticated doctrine of maximum satisfaction which asserted that under competition, and putting aside any quarrels with the distribution of resources among families, competition led to a maximum of satisfaction of the members of an economy. No redistribution of goods among individuals was possible which would benefit even one person without injuring someone else, and similarly the production of any one type of goods could be increased only by decreasing the production of some other type.

If the theorem of maximum satisfaction were literally true, the state would have only two obvious economic functions. The first would be to insure as best it could the condition of competition, for the theorem is easily shown to fail when monopoly is present and powerful. The second would be to alter the distribution of income—at a minimum by caring for persons who owned no income-producing resources, at a maximum by pursuing full egalitarianism. In addition, the state would preserve order and enforce contracts: these tasks devolve on the state primarily because they tend toward monopoly and anyone who controls the army and the courts *is* the government. But then there would be no need for labor legislation, consumer protection laws, farm programs, or any other of the immense number and variety of economic activities now performed by states.

This smug doctrine could not fail to raise the critical hackles of that race of clever and, by self-admission, humane men who occupy themselves as economic theorists. The search for flaws in the doctrine, or, differently put, for the conditions necessary to make it rigorously true, has attracted the attention of this race for more than a century, and time has not tarnished the medals which are bestowed upon the discoverer of a new exception. Let us review their main accomplishments, which may be subsumed under the three headings of externalities, public goods, and erroneous decisions.

EXTERNALITIES

An external effect of an economic decision is an effect, whether beneficial or harmful, upon a person who was not a party to the decision. If my neighbor's carelessness in storing gasoline causes my house to burn, and he does not compensate me, this is an externality of his decision. If the parties to a decision do not reckon in the costs which will fall on others, they may undertake activities which are harmful from the viewpoint of society as a whole. If the parties to a decision do not reckon in benefits which accrue to others, they may spurn activities which would be socially advantageous. Private decisions will not lead to a maximum of satisfaction unless externalities are negligible; or, to use essentially equivalent language, resources are not used with maximum efficiency unless all the results, good and bad, of an investment (that is, its marginal social product)accrue to the person making the investment.

The first systematic account of externalities was undertaken in 1912 by Professor A. C. Pigou. The Pigovian analysis has since been refined to levels of purity exceeding those once proclaimed for Ivory soap, but his immensely influential exposition has not been improved upon with respect to the issues I wish to discuss. But first let us briefly review his treatment.

Pigou divided into three classes the individuals who might be affected by an economic decision. The first class was the owners of durable productive instruments such as land. A tenant would not make an improvement which would last beyond his lease because the landlord, not the tenant, would benefit from its usefulness after the lease expired. I shall ignore this class of discrepancies between private (tenant) and social (tenant plus landlord) products after one remark: if you ask why the lease is not written by the transacting parties to overcome this problem, properly compensating the tenant for the improvement, I give two answers. The first is, of course they will, unless it isn't worth the trouble. The second is, Queen Victoria's Parliament was much exercised with this perhaps nonexistent problem for decades and passed laws seeking to ameliorate the tenant's situation.

Pigou's third class of individuals—I postpone for a moment the second class—affected by decisions were other persons in the same industry, fellow producers (or consumers). A simple example will illustrate the problem here. Suppose I import skilled workers and some subsequently leave me to work for a rival, the next time I will not import so many as would be desirable and even profitable if my rival would bear his share of their transportation costs. A more common example arises when my purchases of some input allow the producer to lower its price to my rivals as well as myself—I take no account of the benefit to them. Industries whose costs fall when their output expands are generally too small under competition, and industries whose costs rise with output are sometimes too large (the two kinds of industry are not strictly symmetrical for reasons we need not discuss).

We are left with Pigou's second class—those instances in which part of the effects of an investment fall on someone other than a landlord or a rival. This is indeed a grab-bag; the following are illustrative Pigovian externalities:

—a monopoly ignores certain burdens it imposes on its customers;

—a lighthouse cannot collect from each ship it guides;

—a discoverer of a basic scientific law cannot collect all the benefits it confers;

—the liquor industry does not have to pay for the policemen and prisons its customers employ;

—so-called competitive advertising;

—"the crowning illustration" is the damage done to their children by pregnant women working in factories, a case complicated by Pigou's observation that if they do not work in factories, poverty may do even more damage.

The Pigovian analysis—and here the later literature goes little further—does not really produce a system for discovering where private economic decisions throw important benefits or costs upon persons outside the decision process. Pigou has two important, overlapping classes of externalities for which one could systematically search: monopolies and decreasing cost industries. The remainder come from anywhere and everywhere, and they are more likely to be identified and publicized by a Ralph Nader than by a professional economist.

Neither Pigou, nor his followers for forty-nine years, ever asked a question which in retrospect is obvious enough: why does not the factory owner negotiate with the housewives whose homes are dirtied by the chimney smoke? The mostly implicit answer was that "technically" this negotiation was not feasible, but of course feasibility is a prime subject for economic study, not a prohibition on investigation. In 1961 Ronald Coase published his great article, "The Problem of Social Cost" (*Journal of Law and Economics*), in which he explained the failure to consult all affected parties to an economic decision by the costs of transactions—the costs of acquiring information, negotiating with parties, and enforcing contracts. Surely this simple reformulation marked a major advance: the economist could systematically study the factors which determined which transactions were feasible and which were not.

Coase asserted an almost incredible proposition: if transaction costs were zero, the theorem on maximum satisfaction would always hold, no matter how the rights and duties of parties were assigned by the law. Whether the factory owner or the housewives were responsible for the damage done to laundry by chimney soot, exactly the socially optimum amount of soot would be produced. Whether the automobile driver or the pedestrian was liable for injury to the latter, each would take the socially optimum amount of care to avoid accidents. In this regime of zero transaction costs, no monopoly would restrict output below the optimum level because consumers would pay the monopolist not to do so. Such miraculous corollaries of the Coase theorem have greatly enlivened an early week in courses in economic theory.

PUBLIC GOODS

A pure public good is defined as any commodity or service which can be used by one person without interfering with the use of the very same service by other persons. The prototype of a public good is national defense: the protection to my neighbor from any known type of attack does not reduce the protection to me. Another example would be a piece of fundamental knowledge: my neighbor's utilization of a mathematical theorem or a new physical principle in no way interferes with my use of them. Although the class of public goods has a long history in economic and political literature, the concept was first formalized in explicit terms by Paul Samuelson as recently as 1954 (*The Review of Economics and Statistics*).

Even with well-functioning competition, the market cannot supply the proper amounts of a public good. The supply of a public good will usually be monopolistic because it does not cost more to supply 5000 people than to supply 500. Therefore, the known inefficiencies of private monopoly are unavoidable if the public good (whether an air force or a scientific discovery or a fire department) is provided privately.

The monopoly element, however, will often be of negligible importance. For example: only one station can broadcast on a given television channel, and the reception of the broadcast by one household does not interfere with the reception of another household, so it is a public good. With predictable advances in technology, however, there could be a hundred different television channels in a city, and none would have monopoly power.

There is a second difficulty with public goods. If my neighbors pay for such a good, it will be freely available to me. Hence I have an incentive to understate my desire for the good—for example, to say that the national defense system or the television broadcast is not of the slightest interest to me, or worth at most $1 a year. With everyone similarly motivated to understate his demand price, the good will be supplied in inadequate quantity. Hence the state must undertake the provision of the public good and finance it with a tax.

Again the market failure is not invariable. The television broadcast could be scrambled, and only the viewer with an unscrambling device could view it. Then it would be of no avail to me to pretend that the broadcast was of less value than the fee: the situation would be exactly the same as if I told the automobile dealer that a new car was not worth its full price to me. The dealer would recommend a bicycle; the television station would commend the Carnegie Public Library. The policing of the use of a public good could be so expensive, however, that it was simply out of question, and then the market failure would be complete.

We may note that if the market could exclude any consumer from a public good without cost (so that the TV scrambler was free) and if the demands of consumers could be accurately ascertained (so that the "free rider" could not sponge off of others), the market would supply the optimum amount of public goods as well as private goods.

ERRONEOUS DECISIONS

Even when all goods are private, and externalities do not exist, there is a third class of market failures. When individuals choose inappropriate means to fulfill their desires, clearly they are not maximizing their satisfactions. There has been no shortage of allegations of such ignorance.

Pigou believed that for articles of wide consumption the price of an article measured well both the desire for the article and the satisfaction obtained from it.

To this general conclusion, however, there is one important exception.

> This exception has to do with people's attitude toward the future. Generally speaking, everybody prefers present pleasures or satisfactions of given magnitude to future pleasures or satisfactions of equal magnitude, even when the latter are perfectly certain to occur. . . . This reveals a far-reaching economic disharmony. For it implies people distribute their resources between the present, the near future and the remote future on the basis of a wholly irrational preference. (*The Economics of Welfare*, 4th ed. [New York, 1932], pp. 24–25)

This one irrationality was serious enough, for it implied that private markets would not conserve resources in proper degree.

The list of alleged failures of the market to bring satisfactions commensurate with expectations was already a long one when Pigou wrote. Consider just three examples:

1. Workmen did not properly appraise the risks of injury or death in their employment, and therefore did not receive sufficiently high wages in risky fields. The law of workman's compensation was presumably based on this view of the labor markets.

2. Individuals were incompetent in choosing doctors, lawyers, pharmacists, and so forth, so the state licensed practitioners to insure that they met minimum levels of competence and responsibility.

3. Individuals were incompetent in choosing banks and insurance companies, so these institutions were closely regulated.

Even the articles of everyday consumption, in whose purchase Pigou trusted the average consumer, had fallen under food and drug legislation in the United States by 1907.

To extend this list of areas of economic incompetency would be the easiest of sports. Airlines would not choose good pilots, so the FAA licenses them. Investors would buy worthless securities, so the SEC insists upon full disclosure of facts. Households would live in unsafe dwellings if the building code did not protect them. Drivers would pilot needlessly dangerous automobiles if left to their own devices. The very clothing we wear would be flammable and shoddy in the absence of protective federal legislation.

One characteristic of these market failures is that they represent more than imperfect knowledge, since all knowledge is imperfect. The protected individuals would not, of their own volition, acquire a proper amount of information, even though one can buy information at its cost of production. I could hire a corporation to choose competent doctors (if the American Medical Association would allow it), just as I hire a university to choose competent professors to instruct my children. I could patronize a store which guaranteed its products, and thus delegate to the store the task of testing quality. The irrationality consists of the underinvestment in information.

A second characteristic is that these failures involve nonfulfillment of the individual's own desires, not any censorship of these desires. When the society forbids children to be chimney sweeps or forbids the public sale of heroin, it is not countering market failure but seeking to thwart the market's fulfillment of undesirable desires. We have a good deal of censorship, and, whether it is good or bad, in each case it is a noneconomic source of state activity.

Market Failures as a Basis for Policy

These three types of "market failures" provide the agenda for the state in economic life, according to welfare economics. The externalities, the public goods, and the incompetences of individuals each allow an improvement in economic affairs to be achieved by an intelligent and efficient government. Yet these three classes of actions never developed into even a partial theory of the economic functions of the state. The literature in each area showed an almost perfect immunity to progress in this respect.

A useful theory of market failure should tell us in what classes of economic activity the market failures occur. Consider the class of incompetent decisions of consumers. What types of goods and services does the consumer usually purchase mistakenly or inefficiently? Is it new products, or physically dangerous goods, or goods purchased infrequently, or goods purchased in small amounts, or goods whose baneful effects are delayed in time? The answer is, unfortunately, that the economist has *no* knowledge of when the consumer is incompetent—he accepts the allegations of a Samuel Plimsoll or Upton Sinclair or Stuart Chase or John Galbraith or Ralph Nader, provided they are accepted by the community at large. No economic analysis has been made of the average error in consumer decisions in different types of decisions.

Much the same thing can be said about each of the other classes of market failures.

If one wishes to learn what the leading externalities are, he should consult, again, not his economist but his reformer. Any far-flung benefits of education which call for public subsidy were not discovered or measured by economists, and the same can be said of investment in research, the problem of neighborhood deterioration, and the problem of congestion. The one important class of exceptions is the set of externalities which arise from monopoly. Whatever his success, the economist has at least tried to locate probable areas of monopoly and examine the consequences of monopoly. Monopoly aside, however, there is no method in economics of predicting where externalities will arise or whether they will be worth talking about.

Finally, public goods are again a category which is presented to the economist. His achievement has been not to determine whether national defense is a public good, but only to show—in a general way—that private provision of national defense will lead to less defense than the citizens (of this country) desire. This is a thoroughly unattractive role which is assigned to the economist: he does not tell the society what to do in the area of economic policy, but merely draws intricate diagrams to explain why the state undertakes what economic functions it happens to undertake. Yet it is his inevitable role so long as he views the economic functions of the state as the performance of those activities which are not performed satisfactorily by the market. How could an economist discover previously neglected externalities? His usual guide is the market, and here by the very nature of the problem the market gives no information: monopoly aside, there are no transactions in externalities; and there are few public goods which are provided privately.

A partial exception to this unwelcome conclusion can be made for consumer incompetence. The market does reveal certain classes of incompetence. The allegation that the labor market is poorly informed and demands public employment exchanges can be tested with data on the dispersion of wage rates. The allegation that a consumer is defrauded *in his own eyes* can be tested by his subsequent purchases. The allegation that consumers buy too few automobile safety devices can be tested by standard research techniques.

In short, even the most diligent and imaginative economists could play only a limited role in the detection of market failures, and those of us who have fallen short of perfection have been of negligible assistance in this role.

THE COMPETENCE OF THE STATE

Let us start afresh. We have a list, a long list, of market failures. They should be corrected if possible, and there are only two alternatives to the market: the state, and prayer. It turns out that the two were merged in one.

We have remarked on the double view of the state held by economists. The one view is a reading of historical reality—perhaps not a systematic or comprehensive reading, but nevertheless one based on empirical observation. Ask Professors Arrow and Samuelson what they think of the U.S. Post Office. I have not asked, so I must predict the answer: my prediction is that these eminent welfare economists will make comments which fall between indignation and resignation but never approach praise. Furthermore, no respectable welfare or nonwelfare economist will praise the state usury laws which prevent school boards from borrowing money, nor will he praise the achievements of the Interstate Commerce Commission in developing an efficient transportation system in the United States.

We are all acutely aware of the imperfectibility of the political system, of its susceptibility to the well-placed minority, of its tardiness in adopting new technologies, of the bureaus that are forgotten islands of indolence, of the carelessness (or worse) of the public's rights by eminent politicians in advancing their private fortunes. We are all aware, too, that the state has at times been ferociously cruel and vindictive in the treatment of unpopular minorities and causes—we surely need look no farther back than the World War II treatment of the Japanese in California.

The second view of the state is that dictated by the *necessities* of optimal economic organization: an institution of noble goals and irresistible means. Consider this passage from Oskar Lange:

> An economic system based upon private enterprise can take but very imperfect account of the alternatives sacrificed and realized in production. Most important alternatives, like life, security, and health of the workers, are sacrificed with-

out being accounted for as a cost of production. A socialist economy would be able to put *all* the alternatives into its economic accounting. (*On the Economic Theory of Social-ism*, ed. B. E. Lippincott [Minneapolis: University of Minnesota Press, 1938], p. 104).

This last sentence would not lose content or meaning if Lange had written: "Almighty Jehovah would be able to put *all* the alternatives into his economic accounting."

Or return to Pigou:

It is plain that divergences between private and social net product ... cannot, like divergences due to tenancy laws, be mitigated by a modification of the contractual relation between any two contracting parties, because the divergence arises out of a service or disservice rendered to persons other than the contracting parties. It is, however, possible for the State, if it so chooses, to remove the divergence in any field by "extraordinary encouragements" or "extraordinary restraints" upon investments in that field. (*The Economics of Welfare*, 4th ed., p. 192)

Again there would be no loss in content, and perhaps some gain in form, if the last sentence were rewritten: "It is, however, ridiculously simple for his Serene Omnipotence, if it pleases him, to remove the divergence in any field by 'extraordinary encour-agements' or 'extraordinary restraints' upon investments in that field."

Neither the cynicism of the first view of the state nor the unreasoning optimism of the second view provides a basis on which the economist can make responsible policy recommen-dations. We may tell the society to jump out of the market frying pan, but we have no basis for predicting whether it will land in the fire or a luxurious bed.

8 The Theory of Economic Regulation

The state—the machinery and power of the state—is a potential
resource or threat to every industry in the society. With its power
to prohibit or compel, to take or give money, the state can and
does selectively help or hurt a vast number of industries. That
political juggernaut, the petroleum industry, is an immense
consumer of political benefits, and simultaneously the underwriters of marine insurance have their more modest repast. The
central tasks of the theory of economic regulation are to explain
who will receive the benefits or burdens of regulation, what form
regulation will take, and the effects of regulation upon the
allocation of resources.

Regulation may be actively sought by an industry, or it may be
thrust upon it. A central thesis of this paper is that, as a rule,
regulation is acquired by the industry and is designed and
operated primarily for its benefit. There are regulations whose
net effects upon the regulated industry are undeniably onerous; a
simple example is the differentially heavy taxation of the industry's product (whiskey, playing cards). These onerous regulations,
however, are exceptional and can be explained by the same theory
that explains beneficial (we may call it "acquired") regulation.

Two main alternative views of the regulation of industry are
widely held. The first is that regulation is instituted primarily for
the protection and benefit of the public at large or some large
subclass of the public. In this view, the regulations which injure
the public—as when the oil import quotas increase the cost of
petroleum products to America by $5 billion or more a year—are
costs of some social goal (here, national defense) or, occasionally,
perversions of the regulatory philosophy. The second view is
essentially that the political process defies rational explanation:
"politics" is an imponderable, a constantly and unpredictably
shifting mixture of forces of the most diverse nature, compre-
hending acts of great moral virtue (the emancipation of slaves)

Reprinted by permission from the *Bell Journal of Economics and
Management Science* (Spring 1971).

and of the most vulgar venality (the congressman feathering his own nest).

Let us consider a problem posed by the oil import quota system: why does not the powerful industry which obtained this expensive program instead choose direct cash subsidies from the public treasury? The "protection of the public" theory of regulation must say that the choice of import quotas is dictated by the concern of the federal government for an adequate domestic supply of petroleum in the event of war—a remark calculated to elicit uproarious laughter at the Petroleum Club. Such laughter aside, if national defense were the goal of the quotas, a tariff would be a more economical instrument of policy: it would retain the profits of exclusion for the treasury. The nonrationalist view would explain the policy by the inability of consumers to measure the cost to them of the import quotas, and hence their willingness to pay $5 billion in higher prices rather than the $3.5 billion in cash that would be equally attractive to the industry. Our profit-maximizing theory says that the explanation lies in a different direction: the present members of the refining industries would have to share a cash subsidy with all new entrants into the refining industry.[1] Only when the elasticity of supply of an industry is small will the industry prefer cash to controls over entry or output.

This question—why does an industry solicit the coercive powers of the state rather than its cash—is offered only to illustrate the approach of the present paper. We assume that political systems are rationally devised and rationally employed, which is to say that they are appropriate instruments for the fulfillment of desires of members of the society. This is not to say that the state will serve any persons's concept of the public interest: indeed the problem of regulation is the problem of discovering when and why an industry (or other group of likeminded people) is able to use the state for its purposes, or is singled out by the state to be used for alien purposes.

WHAT BENEFITS CAN A STATE PROVIDE TO AN INDUSTRY?

The state has one basic resource which in pure principle is not shared with even the mightiest of its citizens: the power to coerce. The state can seize money by the only method which is permitted by the laws of a civilized society, by taxation. The state can ordain the physical movements of resources and the economic decisions of households and firms without their consent. These powers provide the possibilities for the utilization of the state by an industry to increase its profitability. The main policies which an industry (or occupation) may seek of the state are four.

The most obvious contribution that a group may seek of the government is a direct subsidy of money. The domestic airlines received "air mail" subsidies (even if they did not carry mail) of $1.5 billion through 1968. The merchant marine has received construction and operation subsidies reaching almost $3 billion since World War II. The education industry has long shown a masterful skill in obtaining public funds: for example, universities and colleges have received federal funds exceeding $3 billion annually in recent years, as well as subsidized loans for dormitories and other construction. The veterans of wars have often received direct cash bonuses.

We have already sketched the main explanation for the fact that an industry with power to obtain governmental favors usually does not use this power to get money: unless the list of beneficiaries can be limited by an acceptable device, whatever amount of subsidies the industry can obtain will be dissipated among a growing number of rivals. The airlines quickly moved away from competitive bidding for air mail contracts to avoid this problem (see L. S. Keyes, *Federal Control of Entry into Air Transportation* [Cambridge, Mass.: Harvard University Press, 1951], pp. 60 ff.). On the other hand, the premier universities have not devised a method of excluding other claimants for research funds, and in the long run they will receive much-reduced shares of federal research funds.

The second major public resource commonly sought by an industry is control over entry by new rivals. There is considerable, not to say excessive, discussion in economic literature of the rise of peculiar price policies (limit prices), vertical integration, and similar devices to retard the rate of entry of new firms into oligopolistic industries. Such devices are vastly less efficacious (economical) than the certificate of convenience and necessity (which includes, of course, the import and production quotas of the oil and tobacco industries).

The diligence with which the power of control over entry will be exercised by a regulatory body is already well known. The Civil Aeronautics Board has not allowed a single new trunk line to be launched since it was created in 1938. The power to insure new banks has been used by the Federal Deposit Insurance Corporation to reduce the rate of entry into commercial banking by 60 percent (see S. Peltzman, "Entry in Commercial Banking," *Journal of Law and Economics*, October 1965). The interstate motor carrier history is in some respects even more striking, because no even ostensibly respectable case for restriction on entry can be developed on grounds of scale economies (which are in turn adduced to limit entry for safety or economy of operation). The number of federally licensed common carriers is shown in figure 1: the immense growth of the freight hauled by trucking common carriers has been associated with a steady secular decline of

FIGURE 1

CERTIFICATES FOR INTERSTATE MOTOR CARRIERS

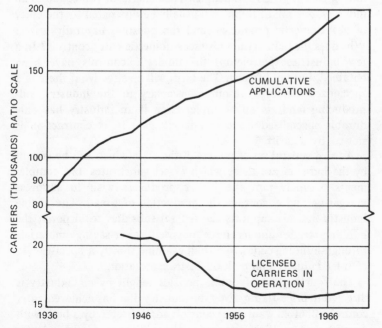

SOURCE: TABLE 5

numbers of such carriers. The number of applications for new certificates has been in excess of 5,000 annually in recent years: a rigorous proof that hope springs eternal in an aspiring trucker's breast.

We propose the general hypothesis: every industry or occupation that has enough political power to utilize the state will seek to control entry. In addition, the regulatory policy will often be so fashioned as to retard the rate of growth of new firms. For example, no new savings and loan company may pay a dividend rate higher than that prevailing in the community in its endeavors to attract deposits. [2] The power to limit the selling expenses of mutual funds, which is soon to be conferred upon the Securities and Exchange Commission, will serve to limit the growth of small mutual funds and hence reduce the sales costs of large funds.

One variant of the control of entry is the protective tariff (and the corresponding barriers which have been raised to interstate movements of goods and people). The benefits of protection to an industry, one might think, will usually be dissipated by the entry of new domestic producers, and the question naturally arises: Why does the industry not also seek domestic entry controls? In a few industries (petroleum) the domestic controls have been obtained, but not in most. The tariff will be effective if there is a specialized domestic resource necessary to the industry; oil-producing lands is an example. Even if an industry has only durable specialized resources, it will gain if its contraction is slowed by a tariff.

A third general set of powers of the state which will be sought by the industry are those which affect substitutes and complements. Crudely put, the butter producers wish to suppress margarine and encourage the production of bread. The airline industry actively supports the federal subsidies to airports; the building trade unions have opposed labor-saving materials through building codes. We shall examine shortly a specific case of inter-industry competition in transportation.

The fourth class of public policies sought by an industry is directed to price-fixing. Even the industry that has achieved entry control will often want price controls administered by a body with coercive powers. If the number of firms in the regulated industry is even moderately large, price discrimination will be difficult to maintain in the absence of public support. The prohibition of interest on demand deposits, which is probably effective in preventing interest payments to most non-business depositors, is a case in point. Where there are no diseconomies of large scale for the individual firm (e.g., a motor trucking firm can add trucks under a given license as common carrier), price control is essential to achieve more than competitive rates of return.

Limitations upon
Political Benefits

These various political boons are not obtained by the industry in a pure profit-maximizing form. The political process erects certain limitations upon the exercise of cartel policies by an industry. These limitations are of three sorts.

First, the distribution of control of the industry among the firms in the industry is changed. In an unregulated industry each firm's influence upon price and output is proportional to its share of industry output (at least in a simple arithmetic sense of direct capacity to change output). The political decisions take account also of the political strength of the various firms, so small firms have a larger influence than they would possess in an unregulated industry. Thus, when quotas are given to firms, the small firms will almost always receive larger quotas than cost-minimizing practices would allow. The original quotas under the oil import quota system will illustrate this practice (table 1). The smallest refiners were given a quota of 11.4 percent of their daily consumption of oil, and the percentage dropped as refinery size rose.[3] The pattern of regressive benefits is characteristic of public controls in industries with numerous firms.

Second, the procedural safeguards required of public processes are costly. The delays which are dictated by both law and bureaucratic thoughts of self-survival can be large: Robert Gerwig found the price of gas sold in interstate commerce to be 5 to 6 percent higher than in intrastate commerce because of the administrative costs (including delay) of Federal Power Commission reviews ("Natural Gas Production: A Study of Costs of Regulation," *Journal of Law and Economics*, October 1962, pp. 69–92).

TABLE 1

IMPORT QUOTAS OF REFINERIES AS PERCENT
OF DAILY INPUT OF PETROLEUM
(Districts I-IV, July 1, 1959-Dec. 31, 1959)

SIZE OF REFINERY (Thousands of Barrels)	PERCENT QUOTA
0-10	11.4
10-20	10.4
20-30	9.5
30-60	8.5
60-100	7.6
100-150	6.6
150-200	5.7
200-300	4.7
300 and over	3.8

Source: Hearing, Select Committee on Small Business, U.S. Congress, 88th Cong., 2nd Sess., Aug. 10 and 11, 1964, [12] p. 121.

Finally, the political process automatically admits powerful outsiders to the industry's councils. It is well known that the allocation of television channels among communities does not maximize industry revenue but reflects pressures to serve many smaller communities. The abandonment of an unprofitable rail line is an even more notorious area of outsider participation.

These limitations are predictable, and they must all enter into the calculus of the profitability of regulation of an industry.

An Illustrative Analysis

The recourse to the regulatory process is of course more specific and more complex than the foregoing sketch suggests. The defensive power of various other industries which are affected by the proposed regulation must also be taken into account. An analysis of one aspect of the regulation of motor trucking will illustrate these complications. At this stage we are concerned only with the correspondence between regulations and economic interests; later we shall consider the political process by which regulation is achieved.

The motor trucking industry operated almost exclusively within cities before 1925, in good part because neither powerful trucks nor good roads were available for long-distance freight movements. As these deficiencies were gradually remedied, the share of trucks in intercity freight movements began to rise, and by 1930 it was estimated to be 4 percent of ton-miles of intercity freight. The railroad industry took early cognizance of this emerging competitor, and one of the methods by which trucking was combatted was state regulation.

By the early 1930s all states regulated the dimensions and weight of trucks. The weight limitations were a much more pervasive control over trucking than the licensing of common carriers because even the trucks exempt form entry regulation are subject to the limitations on dimensions and capacity. The weight regulations in the early 1930s are reproduced in the appendix (table 6). Sometimes the participation of railroads in the regulatory process was incontrovertible: Texas and Louisiana placed a 7,000-pound payload limit on trucks serving (and hence competing with) two or more railroad stations, and a 14,000-pound limit on trucks serving only one station (hence, not competing with it).

We seek to determine the pattern of weight limits on trucks that would emerge in response to the economic interests of the concerned parties. The main considerations appear to be the following:

1. Heavy trucks would be allowed in states with a substantial number of trucks on farms: the powerful agricultural interests would insist upon this. The 1930 Census reports nearly one million trucks on farms. One variable in our study will be, for each state, trucks per 1000 of agricultural population.[4]

2. Railroads found the truck an effective and rapidly triumphing competitor in the shorter hauls and hauls of less than carload traffic, but much less effective in the carload and longer-haul traffic. Our second variable for each state is, therefore, length of average railroad haul.[5] The longer the average rail haul is, the less the railroads will be opposed to trucks.

3. The public at large would be concerned by the potential damage done to the highway system by heavy trucks. The better the state highway system, the heavier the trucks that would be permitted. The percentage of each state's highways that had a high type surface is the third variable. Of course good highways are more likely to exist where the potential contribution of trucks to a state's economy is greater, so the causation may be looked at from either direction.

We have two measures of weight limits on trucks, one for

4-wheel trucks (X_1) and one for 6-wheel trucks (X_2). We may then calculate two equations,

$$X_1 \text{ (or } X_2) = a + bX_3 + cX_4 + dX_5,$$

where

X_3 = trucks per 1000 agricultural labor force, 1930,

X_4 = average length of railroad haul of freight traffic, 1930

X_5 = percentage of state roads with high quality surface, 1930.

(All variables are fully defined and their state values given in table 7 in the appendix).

The three explanatory variables are statistically significant, and each works in the expected direction. The regulations on weight were less onerous; the larger the truck population in farming, the less competitive the trucks were to railroads (i.e., the longer the rail hauls), and the better the highway system (see table 2).

TABLE 2

REGRESSION ANALYSIS OF STATE WEIGHT LIMITS ON TRUCKS
(T values given in parentheses)

DEPENDENT VARIABLE	N	CONSTANT	X_3	X_4	X_5	R^2
X_1	48	12.28 (4.87)	0.0336 (3.99)	0.0287 (2.77)	0.2641 (3.04)	0.502
X_2	46	10.34 (1.57)	0.0437 (2.01)	0.0788 (2.97)	0.2528 (1.15)	0.243

X_1 = Weight limit on 4-wheel trucks (thousands of pounds), 1932-33

X_2 = Weight limit on 6-wheel trucks (thousands of pounds), 1932-33

X_3 = Trucks on farms per 1,000 agricultural labor force, 1930

X_4 = Average length of railroad haul of freight (miles), 1930

X_5 = Percent of state highways with high-type surface, Dec. 31, 1930

Sources: X_1 and X_2: The Motor Truck Red Book and Directory [11], 1934 edition, p. 85-102, and U.S. Dept. of Agric., Bur. of Public Roads, Dec. 1932 [13].

X_3: U.S. Dept. of Commerce, Bureau of the Census, United States Census of Agriculture, 1930, vol. 4 (Washington, D.C.: U.S. Gov't. Printing Office, 1930).

X_4: A.A.R.R., Bur. of Railway Economics, Railway Mileage by States, Dec. 31, 1930 and U.S.I.C.C., Statistics of Railways in the U.S., 1930.

X_5: Statistical Abstract of the U.S., 1932.

The foregoing analysis is concerned with what may be termed the industrial demand for governmental powers. Not every industry will have a significant demand for public assistance (other than money!), meaning the prospect of a substantial increase in the present value of the enterprises even if the governmental services could be obtained gratis (and of course they have costs to which we soon turn). In some economic activities entry of new rivals is extremely difficult to control—consider the enforcement problem in restricting the supply of domestic servants. In some industries the substitute products cannot be efficiently controlled—consider the competition offered to bus lines by private car-pooling. Price fixing is not feasible where every unit of the product has a different quality and price, as in the market for used automobiles. In general, however, most industries will have a positive demand price (schedule) for the services of government.

The Costs of Obtaining Legislation

When an industry receives a grant of power from the state, the benefit to the industry will fall short of the damage to the rest of the community. Even if there were no deadweight losses from acquired regulation, however, one might expect a democratic society to reject such industry requests unless the industry controlled a majority of the votes.[6] A direct and informed vote on oil import quotas would reject the scheme. (If it did not, our theory of rational political processes would be contradicted.) To explain why many industries are able to employ the political machinery to their own ends, we must examine the nature of the political process in a democracy.

A consumer chooses between rail and air travel, for example, by voting with his pocketbook: he patronizes on a given day that mode of transportation he prefers. A similar form of economic voting occurs with decisions on where to work or where to invest one's capital. The market accumulates these economic votes, predicts their future course, and invests accordingly.

Because the political decision is coercive, the decision process is fundamentally different from that of the market. If the public is asked to make a decision between two transportation media comparable to the individual's decision on how to travel—say, whether airlines or railroads should receive a federal subsidy—the decision must be abided by everyone, travelers and non-travelers, travelers this year and travelers next year. This compelled universality of political decisions makes for two differences between democratic political decision processes and market processes.

1. The decisions must be made simultaneously by a large number of persons (or their representatives): the political process demands simultaneity of decision. If A were to vote on the referendum today, B tomorrow, C the day after, and so on, the accumulation of a majority decision would be both expensive and suspect. (A might wish to cast a different vote now than last month.)

The condition of simultaneity imposes a major burden upon the political decision process. It makes voting on specific issues prohibitively expensive: it is a significant cost even to engage in the transaction of buying a plane ticket when I wish to travel; it would be stupendously expensive to me to engage in the physically similar transaction of voting (i.e., patronizing a polling place) whenever a number of my fellow citizens desired to register their views on railroads versus airplanes. To cope with this condition of simultaneity, the voters must employ representatives with wide discretion and must eschew direct expressions of marginal changes in preferences. This characteristic also implies that the political decision does not predict voter desires and make preparations to fulfill them in advance of their realization.

2. The democratic decision process must involve "all" the community, not simply those who are directly concerned with a decision. In a private market, the non-traveler never votes on rail versus plane travel, while the huge shipper casts many votes each day. The political decision process cannot exclude the uninterested voter: the abuses of any exclusion except self-exclusion are obvious. Hence, the political process does not allow participation in proportion to interest and knowledge. In a measure, this difficulty is moderated by other political activities besides voting which do allow a more effective vote to interested parties: persuasion, employment of skilled legislative representatives, and so forth. Nevertheless, the political system does not offer good incentives like those in private markets to the acquisition of

knowledge. If I consume ten times as much of public service A (streets) as of B (schools), I do not have incentives to acquire corresponding amounts of knowledge about the public provision of these services (see G. S. Becker, "Competition and Democracy," *Journal of Law and Economics*, October 1958).

These characteristics of the political process can be modified by having numerous levels of government (so I have somewhat more incentive to learn about local schools than about the whole state school system) and by selective use of direct decision (bond referenda). The chief method of coping with the characteristics, however, is to employ more or less full-time representatives organized in (disciplined by) firms which are called political parties or machines.

The representative and his party are rewarded for their discovery and fulfillment of the political desires of their constituency by success in election and the perquisites of office. If the representative could confidently await reelection whenever he voted against an economic policy that injured the society, he would assuredly do so. Unfortunately virtue does not always command so high a price. If the representative denies ten large industries their special subsidies of money or governmental power, they will dedicate themselves to the election of a more complaisant successor: the stakes are that important. This does not mean that every large industry can get what it wants or all that it wants: it does mean that the representative and his party must find a coalition of voter interests more durable than the anti-industry side of every industry policy proposal. A representative cannot win or keep office with the support of the sum of those who are opposed to: oil import quotas, farm subsidies, airport subsidies, hospital subsidies, unnecessary navy shipyards, an inequitable public housing program, and rural electrification subsidies.

The political decision process has as its dominant characteristic infrequent, universal (in principle) participation, as we have noted: political decisions must be infrequent and they must be global. The voter's expenditure to learn the merits of individual policy proposals and to express his preferences (by individual and group representation as well as by voting) are determined by expected costs and returns, just as they are in the private marketplace. The costs of comprehensive information are higher in the political arena because information must be sought on many issues of little or no direct concern to the individual, and accordingly he will know little about most matters before the legislature. The expressions of preferences in voting will be less precise than the expressions of preferences in the marketplace because many uninformed people will be voting and affecting the decision.[7]

The channels of political decision-making can thus be described as gross or filtered or noisy. If everyone has a negligible preference for policy A over B, the preference will not be discovered or acted upon. If voter group X wants a policy that injures non-X by a small amount, it will not pay non-X to discover this and act against the policy. The system is calculated to implement all strongly felt preferences of majorities and many strongly felt preferences of minorities but to disregard the lesser preferences of majorities and minorities. The filtering of grossness will be reduced by any reduction in the cost to the citizen of acquiring information and expressing desires and by any increase in the probability that his vote will influence policy.

The industry which seeks political power must go to the appropriate seller, the political party. The political party has costs of operation, costs of maintaining an organization and competing in elections. These costs of the political process are viewed excessively narrowly in the literature on the financing of elections: elections are to the political process what merchandising is to the process of producing a commodity, only an essential final step. The party maintains its organization and electoral appeal by the performance of costly services to the voter at all times, not just before elections. Part of the costs of services and organization are borne by putting a part of the party's workers on the public payroll. An opposition party, however, is usually essential insurance for the voters to discipline the party in power, and the opposition party's costs are not fully met by public funds.

The industry which seeks regulation must be prepared to pay with the two things a party needs: votes and resources. The resources may be provided by campaign contributions, contributed services (the businessman heads a fund-raising committee), and more indirect methods such as the employment of party workers. The votes in support of the measure are rallied, and the votes in opposition are dispersed, by expensive programs to educate (or uneducate) members of the industry and of other concerned industries.

These costs of legislation probably increase with the size of the industry seeking the legislation. Larger industries seek programs which cost the society more and arouse more opposition from substantially affected groups. The tasks of persuasion, both within and without the industry, also increase with its size. The fixed size of the political "market," however, probably makes the cost of obtaining legislation increase less rapidly than industry size. The smallest industries are therefore effectively precluded from the political process unless they have some special advantage such as geographical concentration in a sparsely settled political subdivision.

If a political party has in effect a monopoly control over the governmental machine, one might expect that it could collect most of the benefits of regulation for itself. Political parties, however, are perhaps an ideal illustration of Demsetz's theory of natural monopoly ("Why Regulate Utilities?" *Journal of Law and Economics*, April 1968). If one party becomes extortionate (or badly mistaken in its reading of effective desires), it is possible to elect another party which will provide the governmental services at a price more closely proportioned to costs of the party. If entry into politics is effectively controlled, we should expect one-party dominance to lead that party to solicit requests for protective legislation but to exact a higher price for the legislation.

The internal structure of the political party, and the manner in which the perquisites of office are distributed among its members, offer fascinating areas for study in this context. The elective officials are at the pinnacle of the political system—there is no substitute for the ability to hold public office. I conjecture that much of the compensation to the legislative leaders takes the form of extrapolitical payments. Why are so many politicians lawyers?—because everyone employs lawyers, so the congressman's firm is a suitable avenue of compensation, whereas a physician would have to be given bribes rather than patronage. Most enterprises patronize insurance companies and banks, so we may expect that legislators commonly have financial affiliations with such enterprises.

The financing of industry-wide activities such as the pursuit of legislation raises the usual problem of the free rider.[8] We do not possess a satisfactory theory of group behavior—indeed this theory is the theory of oligopoly with one addition: in the very large number industry (e.g., agriculture) the political party itself will undertake the entrepreneurial role in providing favorable legislation. We can go no further than the infirmities of oligopoly theory allow, which is to say, we can make only plausible conjectures such as that the more concentrated the industry, the more resources it can invest in the campaign for legislation.

Occupational Licensing

The licensing of occupations is a possible use of the political process to improve the economic circumstances of a group. The license is an effective barrier to entry because occupational practice without the license is a criminal offense. Since much occupational licensing is performed at the state level, the area provides an opportunity to search for the characteristics of an occupation which give it political power.

Although there are serious data limitations, we may investigate several characteristics of an occupation which should influence its ability to secure political power:

1. *The size of the occupation.* Quite simply, the larger the occupation, the more votes it has. (Under some circumstances, therefore, one would wish to exclude non-citizens from the measure of size.)

2. *The per capita income of the occupation.* The income of the occupation is the product of its number and average income, so this variable and the preceding will reflect the total income of the occupation. The income of the occupation is presumably an index of the probable rewards of successful political action: in the absence of specific knowledge of supply and demand functions, we expect licensing to increase each occupation's equilibrium income by roughly the same proportion. In a more sophisticated version, one would predict that the less the elasticity of demand for the occupation's services, the more profitable licensing would be. One could also view the income of the occupation as a source of funds for political action, but if we view political action as an investment this is relevant only with capital-market imperfections.[9]

The average income of occupational members is an appropriate variable in comparisons among occupations, but it is inappropriate to comparisons of one occupation in various states because real income will be approximately equal (in the absence of regulation) in each state.

3. *The concentration of the occupation in large cities.* When the occupation organizes a campaign to obtain favorable legislation, it incurs expenses in the solicitation of support, and these are higher for a diffused occupation than a concentrated one. The solicitation of support is complicated by the free-rider problem in that individual members cannot be excluded from the benefits of legislation even if they have not shared the costs of receiving it. If most of the occupation is concentrated in a few large centers, these problems (we suspect) are much reduced in intensity: regulation may even begin at the local governmental level. We shall use an orthodox geographical concentration measure: the share of the occupation of the state in cities over 100,000 (or 50,000 in 1900 and earlier).

4. *The presence of a cohesive opposition to licensing.* If an occupation deals with the public at large, the costs which licensing imposes upon any one customer or industry will be small and it will not be economic for that customer or industry to combat the drive for licensure. If the injured group finds it feasible and profitable to act jointly, however, it will oppose the effort to get licensure, and (by increasing its cost) weaken, delay, or prevent the legislation. The same attributes—numbers of voters, wealth, and ease of organization—which favor an occupation in the political arena, of course, favor also any adversary group. Thus, a small occupation employed by only one industry which has few employers will have difficulty in getting licensure; whereas a large occupation serving everyone will encounter no organized opposition.

An introductory statistical analysis of the licensing of select occupations by states is summarized in table 3. In each occupation the dependent variable for each state is the year of first regulation of entry into the occupation. The two independent variables are

1. the ratio of the occupation to the total labor force of the state in the census year nearest to the median year of regulation, and

TABLE 3

INITIAL YEAR OF REGULATION AS A FUNCTION OF RELATIVE SIZE
OF OCCUPATION AND DEGREE OF URBANIZATION

OCCUPATION	NUMBER OF STATES LICENSING	MEDIAN CENSUS YEAR OF LICENSING	REGRESSION COEFFICIENTS (AND T-VALUES)		R^2
			SIZE OF OCCUPATION (RELATIVE TO LABOR FORCE)	URBANIZATION (SHARE OF OCCUPATION IN CITIES OVER 100,000*)	
Beauticians	48	1930	-4.03 (2.50)	5.90 (1.24)	0.125
Architects	47	1930	-24.06 (2.15)	-6.29 (0.84)	0.184
Barbers	46	1930	-1.31 (0.51)	-26.10 (2.37)	0.146
Lawyers	29	1890	-0.26 (0.08)	-65.78 (1.70)	0.102
Physicians	43	1890	0.64 (0.65)	-23.80 (2.69)	0.165
Embalmers	37	1910	3.32 (0.36)	-4.24 (0.44)	0.007
Registered Nurses	48	1910	-2.08 (2.28)	-3.36 (1.06)	0.176
Dentists	48	1900	2.51 (0.44)	-22.94 (2.19)	0.103
Veterinarians	40	1910	-10.69 (1.94)	-37.16 (4.20)	0.329
Chiropractors	48	1930	-17.70 (1.54)	11.69 (1.25)	0.079
Pharmacists	48	1900	-4.19 (1.50)	-6.84 (0.80)	0.082

Sources: The Council of State Governments, "Occupational Licensing Legislation in the States", 1952 and U.S. Census of Population, various years.

*To age between 1900 and 1900.

2. the fraction of the occupation found in cities over 100,000 (over 50,000 in 1890 and 1900) in that same year.

We expect these variables to be negatively associated with year of licensure, and each of the nine statistically significant regression coefficients is of the expected sign.

The results are not robust, however: the multiple correlation coefficients are small, and over half of the regression coefficients are not significant (and in these cases often of inappropriate sign). Urbanization is more strongly associated than size of occupation with licensure.[10] The crudity of the data may be a large source of these disappointments: we measure, for example, the characteristics of the barbers in each state in 1930, but fourteen states were licensing barbers by 1910. If the states which licensed barbering before 1910 had relatively more barbers, or more highly urbanized barbers, the predictions would be improved. The absence of data for years between censuses and before 1890 led us to make only the cruder analysis.[11]

In general, the larger occupations were licensed in earlier years.[12] Veterinarians are the only occupation in this sample who have a well-defined set of customers, namely livestock farmers, and licensing was later in those states with large numbers of livestock relative to rural population. The within-occupation analyses offer some support for the economic theory of the supply of legislation.

A comparison of different occupations allows us to examine several other variables. The first is income, already discussed above. The second is the size of the market. Just as it is impossible to organize an effective labor union in only one part of an integrated market, so it is impossible to regulate only one part of the market. Consider an occupation—junior business executives will do—which has a national market with high mobility of labor and significant mobility of employers. If the executives of one state were to organize, their scope for effective influence would be very small. If salaries were raised above the competitive level, employers would often recruit elsewhere so the demand elasticity would be very high.[13] The third variable is stability of occupational membership: the longer the members are in the occupation, the greater their financial gain from control of entry. Our regrettably crude measure of this variable is based upon the number of members aged 35–44 in 1950 and aged 45–54 in 1960: the closer these numbers are, the more stable the membership of the occupation. The data for the various occupations are given in table 4.

The comparison of licensed and unlicensed occupations is consistently in keeping with our expectations:

1. the licensed occupations have higher incomes (also before licensing, one may assume);

2. the membership of the licensed occupations is more stable (but the difference is negligible in our crude measure);

3. the licensed occupations are less often employed by business enterprises (who have incentives to oppose licensing);

4. all occupations in national markets (college teachers, engineers, scientists, accountants) are unlicensed or only partially licensed.

The size and urbanization of the three groups, however, are unrelated to licensing. The interoccupational comparison therefore provides a modicum of additional support for our theory of regulation.

CONCLUSION

The idealistic view of public regulation is deeply imbedded in professional economic thought. So many economists, for example, have denounced the ICC for its pro-railroad policies that this has become a cliché of the literature. This criticism seems to me exactly as appropriate as a criticism of the Great Atlantic and Pacific Tea Company for selling groceries, or as a criticism of a politician for currying popular support. The fundamental vice of such criticism is that it misdirects attention: it suggests that the way to get an ICC which is not subservient to the carriers is to preach to the commissioners or to the people who appoint the commissioners. The only way to get a different commission would be to change the political support for the Commission, and reward commissioners on a basis unrelated to their services to the carriers.

Until the basic logic of political life is developed, reformers will be ill-equipped to use the state for their reforms, and victims of the pervasive use of the state's support of special groups will be helpless to protect themselves. Economists should quickly estab-

TABLE 4

CHARACTERISTICS OF LICENSED AND UNLICENSED PROFESSIONAL OCCUPATIONS, 1960

OCCUPATION	MEDIAN AGE (Years)	MEDIAN EDUCATION (Years)	MEDIAN EARNINGS (50-52 Weeks)	INSTABILITY OF MEMBERSHIP[*]	PERCENT NOT SELF-EMPLOYED	PERCENT IN CITIES OVER 50,000	PERCENT OF LABOR FORCE
Licensed:							
Architects	41.7	16.8	$ 9,090	0.012	57.8%	44.1%	0.045%
Chiropractors	46.5	16.4	6,360	0.053	5.8	30.8	0.020
Dentists	45.9	17.3	12,200	0.016	9.4	34.5	0.128
Embalmers	43.5	13.4	5,990	0.130	52.8	30.2	0.055
Lawyers	45.3	17.4	10,800	0.041	35.8	43.1	0.308
Prof. Nurses	39.1	13.2	3,850	0.291	91.0	40.6	0.868
Optometrists	41.6	17.0	8,480	0.249	17.5	34.5	0.024
Pharmacists	44.9	16.2	7,230	0.119	62.3	40.0	0.136
Physicians	42.8	17.5	14,200	0.015	35.0	44.7	0.339
Veterinarians	39.2	17.4	9,210	0.169	29.5	14.4	0.023
Average	43.0	16.3	8,741	0.109	39.7	35.7	0.195
Partially Licensed:							
Accountants	40.4	14.9	6,450	0.052	88.1	43.5	0.698
Engineers	38.3	16.2	8,490	0.023	96.8	31.6	1.279
Elem.School Teachers	43.1	16.5	4,710	0.276[a]	99.1	18.8	1.482
Average	40.6	15.9	6,550	0.117[b]	94.7	34.6	1.153
Unlicensed:							
Artists	38.0	14.2	5,920	0.103	77.3	45.7	0.154
Clergymen	43.3	17.0	4,120	0.039	89.0	27.2	0.295
College Teachers	40.3	17.4	7,500	0.085	99.2	36.0	0.261
Draftsmen	31.2	12.9	5,990	0.098	98.6	40.8	0.322
Reporters & Editors	39.4	15.5	6,120	0.138	93.9	43.3	0.151
Musicians	40.2	14.8	3,240	0.081	65.5	37.7	0.289
Natural Scientists	35.9	16.8	7,490	0.264	96.3	32.7	0.221
Average	38.3	15.5	5,768	0.115	88.5	37.6	0.242

[*]1-R, where R = ratio: 1060 age 45 to 54 to 1950 age 35 to 44.

[a]Not available separately; figure here is for Teachers N.E.C. (including secondary school and other).

[b]Includes figure for Teachers N.E.C. in note a.

Source: U.S. Census of Population, 1960.

lish the license to practice on the rational theory of political behavior.

APPENDIX

TABLE 5

COMMON, CONTRACT, AND PASSENGER MOTOR CARRIERS, 1935-1969[a]

YEAR ENDING	CUMULATIVE APPLICATIONS			OPERATING CARRIERS	
	GRAND-FATHER	NEW	TOTAL	APPROVED APPLICATIONS[c]	NUMBER IN OPERATION[b]
Oct. 1936	82,827	1,696	84,523	--	--
1937	83,107	3,921	87,028	1,114	--
1938	85,646	6,694	92,340	20,398	--
1939	86,298	9,636	95,934	23,494	--
1940	87,367	12,965	100,332	25,575	--
1941	88,064	16,325	104,389	26,296	--
1942	88,702	18,977	107,679	26,683	--
1943	89,157	20,007	109,164	27,531	--
1944	89,511	21,324	110,835	27,177	21,044
1945	89,518	22,829	112,347		20,788
1946	89,529	26,392	115,921		20,632
1947	89,552	29,604	119,156		20,665
1948	89,563	32,678	122,241		20,373
1949	89,567	35,635	125,202		18,459
1950	89,573	38,666	128,239		19,200
1951	89,574	41,889	131,463		18,843
1952	(89,574)[d]	44,297	133,870		18,408
1953	"	46,619	136,192		17,869
1954	"	49,146	138,719		17,080
1955	"	51,720	141,293		16,836
June 1956	"	53,640	143,213		16,486
1957	"	56,804	146,377		16,316
1958	"	60,278	149,851		16,065
1959	"	64,171	153,744		15,923
1960	"	69,205	158,778		15,936
1961	"	72,877	162,450		15,967
1962	"	76,986	166,559		15,884
1963	"	81,443	171,016		15,739
1964	"	86,711	176,284		15,732
1965	"	93,064	182,637		15,755
1966	"	101,745	191,318		15,933
1967	"	106,647	196,220		16,003
1968	"	f	f		16,230[e]
1969	"	f	f		16,318[e]

Source: U.S. Interstate Commerce Commission Annual Reports.

[a]Excluding brokers and within-state carriers.

[b]Property carriers were the following percentages of all operating carriers: 1944--93.4%; 1950--92.4%; 1960--93.0%; 1966--93.4%. Number in operation not available prior to 1944.

[c]Estimated.

[d]Not available; assumed to be approximately constant.

[e]1968 and 1969 figures are for number of carriers required to file annual reports.

[f]Not available comparable to previous years; applications for permanent authority *disposed of* (from new and pending files) 1967-69 are as follows: 1967--7,049; 1968--5,724; 1969--5,186.

TABLE 6

WEIGHT LIMITS ON TRUCKS, 1932-33[*], BY STATES (BASIC DATA FOR TABLE 2)

STATE	MAXIMUM WEIGHT (in lbs.)		STATE	MAXIMUM WEIGHT (in lbs.)	
	4-WHEEL[a]	6-WHEEL[b]		4-WHEEL[a]	6-WHEEL[b]
Alabama	20,000	32,000	Nebraska	24,000	40,000
Arizona	22,000	34,000	Nevada	25,000	38,000
Arkansas	22,200	37,000	New Hampshire	20,000	20,000
California	22,000	34,000	New Jersey	30,000	30,000
Colorado	30,000	40,000	New Mexico	27,000	45,000
Connecticut	32,000	40,000	New York	33,600	44,000
Delaware	26,000	38,000	No. Carolina	20,000	20,000
Florida	20,000	20,000	No. Dakota	24,000	48,000
Georgia	22,000	39,600	Ohio	24,000	24,000
Idaho	24,000	40,000	Oklahoma	20,000	20,000
Illinois	24,000	40,000	Oregon	25,500	42,500
Indiana	24,000	40,000	Pennsylvania	26,000	36,000
Iowa	24,000	40,000	Rhode Island	28,000	40,000
Kansas	24,000	34,000	So. Carolina	20,000	25,000
Kentucky	18,000	18,000	So. Dakota	20,000	20,000
Louisiana	13,400	N.A.	Tennessee	20,000	20,000
Maine	18,000	27,000	Texas	13,500	N.A.
Maryland	25,000	40,000	Utah	26,000	34,000
Massachusetts	30,000	30,000	Vermont	20,000	20,000
Michigan	27,000	45,000	Virginia	24,000	35,000
Minnesota	27,000	42,000	Washington	24,000	34,000
Mississippi	18,000	22,000	West Va.	24,000	40,000
Missouri	24,000	24,000	Wisconsin	24,000	36,000
Montana	24,000	34,000	Wyoming	27,000	30,000

[*] Red Book figures are reported (p. 89) as "Based on the state's interpretations of their laws [1933] and on physical limitations of vehicle design and tire capacity." Public Roads figures are reported (p. 167) as "an abstract of state laws, including legislation passed in 1932."

[a] 4-Wheel: The smallest of the following three figures was used:

   (A) Maximum gross weight (as given in Red Book, pp. 90-91).

   (B) Maximum axle weight (as given in Red Book, pp. 90-91), multiplied by 1.5 (see Red Book, p. 89).

   (C) Maximum gross weight (as given in Red Book, p. 93).

   Exceptions: Texas and Louisiana--see Red Book, p. 91.

[b] 6-Wheel: Maximum gross weight as given in Public Roads, p. 167. These figures agree in most cases with those shown in Red Book, p. 93, and with Public Roads maximum axle weights multiplied by 2.5 (see Red Book, p. 93). Texas and Louisiana are excluded as data are not available to convert from payload to gross weight limits.

TABLE 7

INDEPENDENT VARIABLES (BASIC DATA FOR TABLE 2--CONT'D)

STATE	TRUCKS ON FARMS PER 1,000 AGRICULTURAL LABOR FORCE	AVERAGE LENGTH OF RAILROAD HAUL OF FREIGHT(miles)[a]	PERCENT OF STATE HIGHWAYS WITH HIGH-TYPE SURFACE[b]
Alabama	26.05	189.4	1.57
Arizona	79.74	282.2	2.60
Arkansas	28.62	233.1	1.72
California	123.40	264.6	13.10
Colorado	159.50	244.7	0.58
Connecticut	173.80	132.6	7.98
Delaware	173.20	202.7	21.40
Florida	91.41	184.1	8.22
Georgia	32.07	165.7	1.60
Idaho	95.89	243.6	0.73
Illinois	114.70	207.9	9.85
Indiana	120.20	202.8	6.90
Iowa	98.73	233.3	3.39
Kansas	146.70	281.5	0.94
Kentucky	20.05	227.5	1.81
Louisiana	31.27	201.0	1.94
Maine	209.30	120.4	1.87
Maryland	134.20	184.1	12.90
Massachusetts	172.20	144.7	17.70
Michigan	148.40	168.0	6.68
Minnesota	120.40	225.6	1.44
Mississippi	29.62	164.9	1.14
Missouri	54.28	229.7	2.91
Montana	183.80	266.5	0.09
Nebraska	132.10	266.9	0.41
Nevada	139.40	273.2	0.39
New Hampshire	205.40	129.0	3.42
New Jersey	230.20	137.6	23.30
New Mexico	90.46	279.0	0.18
New York	220.50	163.3	21.50
No. Carolina	37.12	171.5	8.61
No. Dakota	126.40	255.1	0.01
Ohio	125.80	194.2	11.20
Oklahoma	78.18	223.3	1.42
Oregon	118.90	246.2	3.35
Pennsylvania	187.60	166.5	9.78
Rhode Island	193.30	131.0	20.40
So. Carolina	20.21	169.8	2.82
So. Dakota	113.40	216.6	0.04
Tennessee	23.98	191.9	3.97
Utah	101.70	235.7	1.69
Vermont	132.20	109.7	2.26
Virginia	71.88	229.8	2.86
Washington	180.90	254.4	4.21
West Virginia	62.88	218.7	8.13
Wisconsin	178.60	195.7	4.57
Wyoming	133.40	286.7	0.08

[a]Average length of RR haul of (revenue) freight = Average distance in miles each ton is carried = Ratio of number of ton-miles to number of tons carried for each state, average length of haul was obtained by weighting average length of haul of each company by the number of miles of line operated by that company in the state (all for class I RR's).

[b]Percentage of state roads with high-quality surface: Where high-quality (high-type) surface consists of bituminous macadam, bituminous concrete, sheet asphalt, Portland cement concrete, and block pavements. All state rural roads, both local and state highways systems, are included.

Supplementary Note on
Economic Theories of
Regulation (1975)

Richard Posner, my esteemed colleague, has raised a variety of
questions about economic theories of regulation in general and
the foregoing essay in particular ("Theories of Economic Regulation," *Bell Journal*, Autumn 1974). The following remarks may
clarify my position.

Special Interests vs.
Public Interests

An underlying theme of Posner's article is that two opposing
theories of the regulation of economic (and, for that matter,
social) affairs must be chosen between: either the regulations are
obtained by special interests or they serve the public interest.

> Another sort of weakness is that the theory [of economic
> regulation], pushed to its logical extreme, becomes rather
> incredible, because it excludes the possibility that a society
> concerned with the ability of interest groups to manipulate
> the political process in their favor might establish institu-
> tions that enabled genuine public interest considerations to
> influence the formation of policy.... One can of course say
> that on some issues the relevant interest group consists of
> everyone, or almost everyone, in the society. But this usage
> robs the interest group concept of its utility by collapsing it
> into the public interest theory. (Ibid., pp. 349–50)

These alternative theories are in fact the same theory: that
people seek to maximize their own utility subject to restraints—
restraints so complex and varied as to provide economists with
indefinite future employment. There is no difference in principle
between my favoring public subsidies to universities to increase
my income (special interest) and to improve the education of
other people's children (public interest)—the only difference is
that there are more people with the latter goal than with the
former.

There is, in fact, only one general theory of human behavior,
and that is the utility-maximizing theory. The only reason for
discussing the political behavior of any one group (say, an
industry) rather than the entire society is the reason for partial

equilibrium analysis: that at the industry level it is possible to specify a set of goals (above all, control over entry of new rivals) that provide substantive content to what would otherwise be purely formal maximizing conditions. That the "public" maximizes its goals is not inconsistent with an industry maximizing its benefits, even when the industry gains and the public loses. Indeed, this exact relationship holds when a private monopolist sells at a profit-maximizing price in a market: it does not pay the consumers, given their costs of joint action, to "buy" the socially optimal marginal-cost price from the monopolist. It no more "robs the interest group concept of its utility," however, to recognize that other interest groups (possibly of vast size) exist, than it robs the theory of monopoly of utility to recognize that consumers also maximize their utility.

The Political Equilibrium of Interest Groups

The economist is accustomed to dealing with a world in which there is a more or less continuous relationship between inputs and outputs, or between efforts and achievements. The political literature, even that written by economists, is pervaded by an all-or-none logic: a party wins an election, or it loses; a law is passed, or it is defeated. I wish to argue that our traditional economic logic is also more appropriate to the political arena.[14]

Thus, it is not correct to say that a producer group—even the most powerful group—gets all that it might wish from the political process. Indeed this proposition is contradicted so long as any producer group with demonstrated access to the political machinery still has a positive marginal utility of money. The political process, like the economic process, finds intermediate positions which reflect the equilibrium of diverse forces.

Let us assume that the political power of a group in the society is a function of the amount of resources (r dollars) it is prepared to devote to a given political-economic issue. The resources will be determined by the profits it can obtain, or the reduction in costs it will obtain through lower buying prices, or the strength of its desire for some other goal. The resources include voting power, and hence depend upon the numerical size of the group. The final political equilibrium will be not that one party or the other "wins" according to whose power is larger, but rather that an intermediate solution will be attained, where—at the margin—the strengths of the two parties are equal.

For example, an industry seeks higher profits by obtaining public control of entry. Its profits (gross of political expenditures) will depend upon the rate of entry (E) of new resources into the industry. The amount of entry restraint the industry will achieve depends upon resources it expends (r_i) and the resources spent by the group that loses from lower entry (r_o), with actual entry being $E = f(r_i, r_o)$. The industry will find the level of political expenditure (r_i) that maximizes its expected *net* profit, and similarly with the other party, say consumers. On a Cournot-type assumption that the expenditures of the other party are given, each group will maximize the present value of its political variables minus the cost of obtaining them.

A central problem of the economic theory of regulation—and it is one which I freely concede has not been solved—is to determine the nature and arguments of the function defining the political power of a group. The theory of coalitions is not well developed, and we do not know the specific effects of various constellations of number and gains (including homogeneity of interests, duration of interests, etc.) upon the political activity and the effective political power of a group. We are reasonably confident that the political resources a group will be able to bring to bear on a proposed policy increase with (1) the total gains the group expects to obtain from the policy, and (2) the larger the average gain per member of the group. (Hence the absolute number of members will have an ambiguous effect since in general the total gain will increase with the size of the group.) But we cannot confidently predict the effects of differences in the distribution of gains among individuals, the effect of different political systems (PR versus single constituencies), etc.

THE PROBLEM OF EVIDENCE

Posner states that the self-interest theory of regulation is "so spongy that virtually any observations can be reconciled with it." This is a misinterpretation of the role of the theory. It is essentially inconceivable (but not impossible) that the theory of utility-maximizing is wrong, and the purpose of empirical investigation is not to test this assumption (pace Friedman).

It is of course true that the theory would be contradicted if, for a given regulatory policy, we found the group with larger benefits and lower costs of political action being dominated by another group with lesser benefits and higher cost of political action. Temporary accidents aside, such cases simply will not arise: our extensive experience with the general theory in economics gives us the confidence that this is so. Indeed there is no alternative hypothesis.

The theory tells us to look, as precisely and carefully as we can, at who gains and who loses, and how much, when we seek to explain a regulatory policy. The mediocre results of studies of which industries receive tariffs and which occupations receive licenses come not from "failures" of the hypothesis but from the extreme crudeness of the measures of benefits and costs. The purposes of the empirical studies are different.[15]

The first purpose of the empirical studies is to identify the purpose of the legislation! The announced goals of a policy are sometimes unrelated or perversely related to its actual effects, and the *truly intended effects should be deduced from the actual effects*. This is not a tautology designed to gloss over a hard problem, but instead a hypothesis on the nature of political life. Policies may of course be adopted in error, and error is an inherent trait of the behavior of men. But errors are not what men live by or on. If an economic policy has been adopted by many communities, or if it is persistently pursued by a society over a long span of time, it is fruitful to assume that the real effects were known and desired. Indeed, an explanation of a policy in terms of error or confusion is no explanation at all—anything and everything is compatible with that "explanation."

The second purpose of the empirical studies is to provide a testing ground for hypotheses on the factors which govern the political force of a group. Suppose that a superbly accurate study revealed that when a particular industry taxed, through regulatory policies, the rest of the society, it achieved a gain of S with a political expenditure of r_i, at the cost of T to a group who spent r_o in opposition. We have then observed a point of equilibrium of political-economic forces, and with sufficient points we can estimate the "political power" function. (The analogy to the studies relating profitability to concentration is obvious, but not heartening.) In fact there will also be other policy variables, and probably manageable proxies for political resources, but the empirical studies will provide the main outline of the determinants of the political power of a group as a function of various characteristics relevant to the political process.

This is admittedly an empirical approach to political power, and it would clearly be preferable to be able to deduce the determinants of the power of a group from a general theory of political process. At least we need not sit idle until such a theory has been constructed. Meanwhile it is illuminating to view the regulatory process as one which always benefits the regulated industry in some respects, and under less than fully defined conditions favorable to the industry (and unfavorable to those outside the industry) the regulatory process benefits primarily that industry.

FIVE

Extensions and Applications

9

The Process of Economic Regulation

The regulatory agency is an inevitable instrument in the public control of industries, occupations, and other particular branches of economic activity. The regulations are usually particular to the activity, and hence call for a measure of specialized knowledge. The specialized agency, however, is as welcome to the regulated activity as it is necessary to the legislature: by constant association and pressure the regulator is brought to a cooperative and even compliant attitude toward the regulated group.

The present essay is devoted to the following aspects of the role of the agency in the regulatory process: (1) the measurement of the amount of regulation, and its relationship to agency expenditures; (2) the growth of regulatory expenditures; (3) the use of fees in regulation; (4) the career patterns of regulatory officials. Even with this emphasis upon procedural rather than substantive aspects of regulation, some results may be gleaned on the rationale of the regulatory process.

THE MEASUREMENT OF THE AMOUNT OF REGULATION

The state imposes innumerable regulations upon its citizens, and we would like to be able to measure their magnitude. Some regulations may simply have no effect at all: for example, a requirement that college professors have an elementary school education would be (let us hope) vacuous. Other regulations must have only trivial effects: for example, the requirement that the director of a corporation own a certain number of ("qualifying") shares in the corporation. Still other regulations have a substantial effect: for example, the permission to operate a TV station in a large city is worth millions of dollars—and the sum can be ascertained from market transactions. We should like to know

Reprinted by permission from the *Antitrust Bulletin* 17, no. 1 (Spring 1972); © 1972 by Federal Legal Publications, Inc., 95 Morton Street, New York, N. Y. 10014.

how much a set of regulations really changes things. The problem
is: which things?

We may specify our problem more closely with a simple
economic example. A monopoly, if left alone, sets a given price
and sells a given quantity of goods per unit of time (see figure 1).
The state now sets a maximum price and enforces it. What are
the effects?

1. The monopolist suffers a decrease in profits, which we can
measure. (It is $BP_m SD$ *minus* $SP_r NT$.)

2. The consumers gain an increment of consumers' surplus,
which again in principle we can measure. (Here it is $P_m P_r S$.)
They also save a certain sum on the quantity of commodity
previously purchased ($BP_m SD$).

3. Resource owners (other than the monopolist) gain from the
expansion of output and consequent increased demand for their
resources. (Here the gain is zero because the resources are wholly
unspecialized—marginal cost is infinitely elastic.)

4. The costs of regulation (enforcement and compliance) are
also measurable in principle. (Here compliance costs are assumed
to be zero—the cost curve was not altered when regulation was
imposed. Enforcement costs borne by the public are not recorded
in the diagram.)

Of course this textbook example is the exact converse of the
typical regulatory situation: the competitive industry uses control
of entry or price-fixing to obtain a monopoly return. Only the
signs of the various quantities are reversed in this more realistic
version.

If we seek a summary number to measure the impact of regulation, welfare economics would suggest that we proceed as follows.
The loss of revenue to the monopolist on his original sales is
exactly cancelled by the savings to buyers on this quantity. (The
error in this correlation is discussed in an article by Richard
Posner, "The Social Cost of Monoploy and Regulation," *Journal
of Political Economy*, 1975.) Putting aside—as economists hastily
do—the question of the optimum distribution of income, we may
neglect this transfer. Hence income rises by the sum of producer
and consumer surplus changes *minus* the costs of enforcement
and regulation. In our example, the regulation increases welfare

Figure 1.

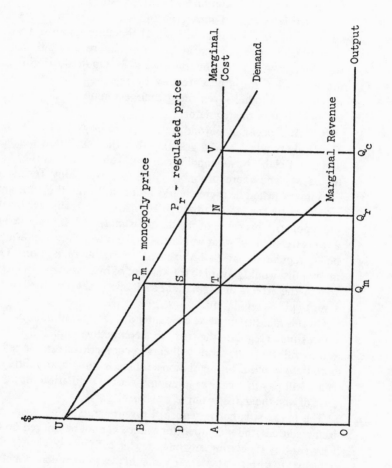

if enforcement and compliance costs are less than the rise in consumers' surplus ($P_mP\ S$) plus the addition to producers' surplus (TSP N). The "cost of the regulation to society is negative! (In the converse case, where the industry obtains a monopoly by regulation, the cost of regulation is of course positive.)

Even this system of measurement, wisely chosen regulations need not be costless or beneficial. If the state imposes a safety regulation, and forces consumers to buy more safety than they wish, wefare—*as judged by consumers*—is impaired.[1] In this case the regulation must be defended by rejecting the consumers' measure of product—replacing their estimate of the value of safety by that of the regulator.

It seems peculiar beyond tolerance to say that a field is negatively regulated, even granting that the regulation was wise and beneficial. The monopolist can truthfully assure us that *he* is regulated, and there probably is no corresponding feeling of consumers (whether there should be or not) that they are anti-regulated by the state (although they are less regulated by the monopolist). This sense of regulation is more or less described by a measure such as: what would the individuals whose behavior is being regulated pay to be excused from the regulation? Our monopolist would pay up to the amount of his loss of profits to be free of the effects of regulation, and this is the measure of the severity of the regulation.

On this measurement we encounter another paradox: it may be impossible to regulate the firms in a competitve industry! In long run equilibrium the firms will earn a competitive rate of return both before and after regulation so there is no amount entrepreneurs will pay to escape regulation.[2] Yet the regulation may even have driven the industry out of existence!

The paradox is not very deep. Entrepreneurs using unspecialized resources under competition indeed cannot be injured (in the long run) by regulating any one area of activity—obviously they will shift to unregulated areas until they earn as much as before in the regulated activity.[3] But consumers do not have perfect alternatives,[4] and they will be injured by the regulation if it imposes changes which they would not freely purchase.

When a regulation accomplishes what the consumers wish, and

this same result could not be achieved by the market, we may still have negative regulation. Thus, let the smoke from chimneys not be subject to market determination because of high transaction costs. A regulation which fixes the smoke at the optimum level will increase consumer surplus, and with smoke produced competitively will have no effect upon factory owners. Negative regulation here means what we would want it to mean: an enlargement of consumer choice.

In summary, the restrictive impact of a regulation can be measured by the reduction it imposes upon consumers or owners of resources. The offsetting benefits of the regulation will not be reckoned in to the measurement of the displacement effect of the regulation, even though they will of course enter into the decision whether the regulation is desirable. In our monopoly example, the reduction of monopoly profits is the measure of the impact on the monopolist, and the maximum regulation is one which eliminates monopoly profits. (Any further regulation would be overkill.) In this same example, the impact upon the consumers is measured by their savings in expenditures due to the price reduction plus the gain in consumer surplus, and this is a negative cost—they would be willing to pay up to this amount for the regulation.[5]

The approach allows us to quantify the impact of regulation upon any class of affected individuals. We can turn the absolute dollar measure of regulation into a relative measure by dividing it by the appropriate total of consumer or producer (including monopoly) surplus. Thus our monopoly measure for producers would be:

$$\frac{\text{Reduction in Monopoly Profit}}{\text{Prior Monopoly Profit}} = \frac{BP_mSD - SP_rNT}{ABP_mT}$$

The relative gain to consumers would be

$$\frac{\text{Savings} + \text{Gain in Consumer Surplus}}{\text{Prior Consumer Surplus}} = \frac{BP_mSD + P_mP_rS}{BUP_m}$$

The denominators should be chosen so relative regulation cannot impose damage exceeding unity, but of course there is no corresponding maximum relative benefit.

Empirical Measures of the
Production of Regulation

The upshot of the preceding remarks is that we can measure the benefits of regulation to the group (consumers or producers, say) who obtain it by the maximum amount they would be willing to pay to obtain it. On the other side, we can in principle measure the inputs necessary to *obtain* and to operate the regulatory system, and speak of a production function of regulation.

As a rather primitive example, consider the scatter diagram (fig. 2) of deflated expenditures of the Antitrust Division relative to the number of cases brought, 1945–69. The supporters of this particular policy are the public at large (consumers), and from the social viewpoint it would be desirable to reckon in the additional expenditures of the regulated firms (those prosecuted, evading or complying with the antitrust laws). These private expenditures are presumably many-fold the public expenditures.[6] The "output" measure, antitrust cases instituted, understates output by excluding pre-merger clearances (which have been rising in number) and perhaps overstates the output (or input) by including a rising fraction of settlements by consent decrees, which are not subsequently litigated.

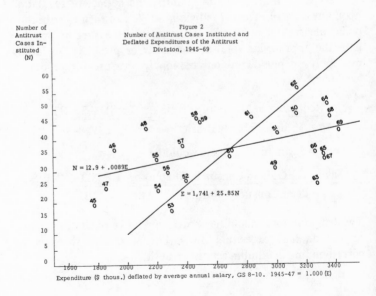

Figure 2
Number of Antitrust Cases Instituted and
Deflated Expenditures of the Antitrust
Division, 1945–69

$N = 12.9 + .0089E$

$E = 1,741 + 25.85N$

Expenditure (\$ thous.) deflated by average annual salary, GS 8–10. 1945–47 = 1.000 (E)

Number of Antitrust Cases Instituted (N)

The scatter diagram suggests that the elasticity of number of cases with respect to expenditures is roughly two-thirds—total deflated expenditures increase 3/2 times the proportion in which the number of antitrust cases increases.[7] It would be possible to measure the importance of individual antitrust cases at least to some extent: data are often available on size of the affected market, and always upon the nature of the offense, the outcome, and the penalties.[8] A measure of the potential "demand" for regulation, the extent of the regulated activity, is discussed in the next section.

A few regulatory bodies report expenditures on a fairly well-defined activity, and these—together with the Antitrust Division—are examined in table 1. In each case the regression is in logarithmic form, so the regression coefficients are also elasticities.[9] In only one agency do we find the measure of activity growing relatively as fast as deflated expenditures.

One is almost invited to suspect that the regulatory bodies seek to avoid such measures of their cost or production functions: they commonly use nonfunctional classifications of expenditures and proliferate their measures of output. The bodies regulating several

TABLE 1

REGRESSIONS OF MEASURES OF REGULATORY OUTPUT UPON EXPENDITURES
(logarithmic form)

AGENCY AND ACTIVITY	PERIOD	ELASTICITY OF ACTIVITY WITH RESPECT TO EXPENDITURES	
Federal Home Loan Bank Bd. Examination of Savings and Loan Associations	1949-69	.47	(t = 16.9)
National Labor Relations Bd. Reports of Trial Examiners	1949-69	1.09	(t = 13.0)
Wage and Hour Division, Department of Labor Investigation of Establishments	1949-69	.76	(t = 7.3)
Interstate Commerce Commission Field Audits of Carrier Accounts	1955-69	-.02	(t = .1)
Antitrust Division Cases Instituted	1945-69	.72	(t = 2.8)

Source: U.S. Bureau of the Budget, Budget of the United States.

areas, such as FCC (TV, radio, telephone) and ICC (rail, trucking, inland waters) seldom classify either expenditures or activities by area. Investigations and cases are never classified by dollar magnitudes involved: always we are given aggregates (thus, 11,927 applications for complaint received by the indolent FTC in 1969 as against 262,892 freight tariffs filed with the busy ICC). The demands for full disclosure from private parties make an interesting contrast to the ubiquitous silences and ambiguities of the regulatory bodies.

THE GROWTH OF REGULATORY EXPENDITURES

The main regulatory agencies and commissions of the Federal Government are listed in table 2, together with data on the growth of their expenditures, and detailed data on selected large regulatory agencies are presented in figure 3. Economic regulation is clearly a prosperous calling: the average federal regulatory agency doubles its dollar expenditures each eight to ten years.

Although the federal regulatory agencies vary greatly in the scope of their operations as well as in age, their expenditure patterns have remarkable similarities:

1. The onslaught of the Great Depression led to substantial decreases in expenditures for only two agencies, the ICC and the Packers and Stockyard Administration; most agencies' expenditures were stable or expanding during this period.

2. During World War II most agencies grew very little, and a few contracted moderately (but two, FCC and CAB, expanded enormously).

3. In the mid-1950s virtually *every* agency entered into a period of sustained and rapid expansion of expenditures. For most agencies retardation set in again in the late 1960s, but no instance of a decrease can be found.

The similarity of movement of expenditures of various regulatory agencies is closer, indeed, than the similarity in the rates of growth of the respective industries they regulate.

Differences in the rate of growth of the regulated industry or activity are in fact of only minor relevance to the differences among agencies' expenditure patterns. The large difference between the growth of aviation and other transportation indus-

TABLE 2

LEVEL AND GROWTH OF EXPENDITURES OF FEDERAL REGULATORY BODIES
AND GROWTH OF REGULATED ACTIVITY

AGENCY	1969* Expenditures (Millions)	Initial Date of Expend. Data[a]	INITIAL DATE TO 1969* EXPENDITURES Annual Rate of Growth[b]	r²[b]	1950 TO 1967* ANNUAL RATES OF GROWTH Expenditures[b]	Regulated Activity[c]
Antitrust Division	$ 8.3	1925	10.0	.91	5.3%	5.0%
Civil Aeronautics Bd.	11.3[d]	1941	9.4[d]	.96	8.2	11.4
FCC	20.7	1929	9.4	.85	6.9	9.1
ICC	27.2[d]	1925	2.8[d]	.65	6.4	2.5
FTC	16.8	1925	6.3	.95	9.0	5.0
Food & Drug Adm.	68.9	1926	8.9	.90	15.9	5.1
Federal Home Loan Bank Bd.	18.9	1944	11.7	.96	14.0	15.3
FPC	15.7	1925	12.4	.86	8.5	7.3
NLRB	34.8	1937	9.2	.94	8.6	0.8
SEC	18.6	1936	4.6	.81	7.7	11.0
Commodity Exchange Auth.	1.9	1925	6.0	.91	4.6	8.2[e]
Wage and Hour Division	25.8	1940	6.7	.93	7.9	1.5
Tariff Commission		1925	3.8	.87	7.0	8.4
Maritime Commission	3.7	1963	8.4	.96	10.3[f]	-2.6[f]
Packer and Stockyards Admn.	2.8	1925	4.6	.76	9.9	3.4

*Unless otherwise specified.

[a]An initial date of 1925 was chosen for agencies established prior to 1925. For other agencies, the first full year of operation was taken as the initial date.

[b]Calculated from the equation, $\log_e(\text{industry size}) = a+bt$; annual rate = $100b$.

[c]Calculated as $(100b)$ from the equation, $\log_e(\text{industry size}) = a+bt$, where size is generally gross receipts; union membership for NLRB; private nonagricultural employment for Wage & Hour Div.; net tonnage in foreign trade for Maritime Commission; val. of imports for Tariff Commission; income originating in manufacturing and trade for Antitrust Division and FTC.

[d]1967 is the terminal year, to maintain historical comparability. On a current reporting basis, the 1969 expenditures were $9.8 for the CAB, and $24.7 for the ICC.

[e]1956-67; earlier data not available.

[f]1963-67.

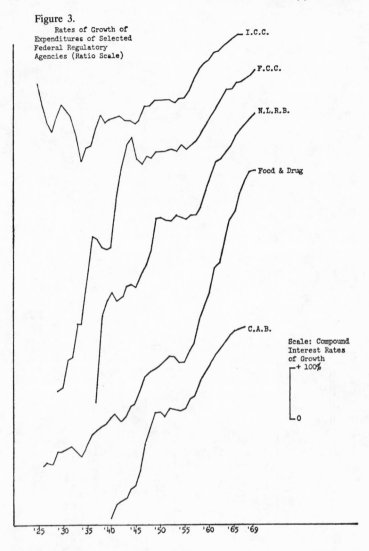

Figure 3.
    Rates of Growth of
Expenditures of Selected
Federal Regulatory
Agencies (Ratio Scale)

I.C.C.

F.C.C.

N.L.R.B.

Food & Drug

C.A.B.

Scale: Compound
Interest Rates
of Growth
+ 100%

0

'25 '30 '35 '40 '45 '50 '55 '60 '65 '69

tries (11.4 percent v. 2.5 percent per year, 1950–67) is associated
with only a modest difference in the growth rates of the CAB and
the ICC (8.2 percent v. 6.4 percent per year). The Antitrust
Division spent $8.3 million in 1969 to combat monopoly through-
out the economy; the FCC spent $20.7 million to supervise radio,
television, and long distance telephone industries; the Food and

Drug Administration an immense $68.9 million to watch only the safety of drugs and foods (excluding meats).[10]

The correspondence between the expenditures of a regulatory body and its area of regulation is better examined by a comparison of regulation of public utilities by the states. In 1966, 36 states had public service commissions which regulated virtually all traditional utilities (railroads, trucking, electricity, gas, water). Per capita expenditures of these public service commissions can be regressed upon state personal income per capita, which should be reasonably well correlated with the total *revenues* of utilities, and upon state public revenues per capita:

$$X_1 = -.111 + .027\, X_2 + 1.75\, X_3$$
$$(t = .42)\quad (t = 2.36)$$

where X_1 = expenditures of the public service commission, per capita,

X_2 = personal income, per capita,

X_3 = state revenues, per capita.

(The results are not changed appreciably if X_2 and X_3 are separately correlated with X_1.) The availability of regulatory funds appears to be a much better predictor of regulatory expenditures than the extent of the economic activity to be regulated.

Considerable economic regulation is performed by state governmental agencies, so a comparable investigation was made of the expenditures of selected Illinois regulatory bodies.[11] The basic data, roughly parallel in form of presentation to that for Federal agencies, is given in table 3 and figure 4.[12] The state pattern differs in several important respects from that of the federal government. The average rate of growth of state expenditures was only half as large as that of the federal agencies, and where the functions roughly overlap (securities, public utilities, aviation, labor), the federal agency's rate of growth always exceeds that of the state. It requires only a moderate time horizon to extrapolate these trends to a date when the state regulatory activities will be negligible in areas in which the federal government is active. The state expenditures were also considerably more responsive to the state of public revenues than the federal expenditures: almost every significant state agency for which we have data—insurance supervision is the exception—underwent a short decline in the Great Depression. The state and federal

TABLE 3

LEVEL AND GROWTH OF EXPENDITURES OF ILLINOIS REGULATORY BODIES AND GROWTH OF REGULATED ACTIVITY

AGENCY	1968 Expenditures (Thousands)	Initial Date of Expend. Data	INITIAL DATE TO 1969 EXPENDITURES		1950 TO 1967* ANNUAL RATES OF GROWTH	
			Annual Rate of Growth	r^2	Expenditures	Regulated Activity**
Aeronautics Com.	$ 574	1932	12.3%	.87	8.1%	1.0%
Bank and Trust Com.	1,125	1955	5.9	.88	5.2	8.5
Illinois Commerce Com.	2,151	1925	3.3	.92	3.8	6.8
Dept. of Fin. Instit. (and Savings and Loan)	1,780	1958	5.0	.78	3.9	8.0
Dept. of Insurance	1,851	1925	4.9	.96	4.2	6.4
Liquor Control Com.	511	1935	2.9	.68	1.5	1.4
Dept. of Mines and Minerals	912	1925	5.3	.88	3.0	1.4
Securities Division (Sec. of State)	179	1958	4.8	.67	2.8	3.2
Dept. of Agriculture, Regulatory Divisions	6,509	1925	3.4	.81	5.7	1.7
Dept. of Labor, Regulatory Divisions	1,127	1925	4.8	.92	2.0	1.3

General note: See Federal Table notes (a), (b), and (c) for method (table 2).

*
With the following exceptions: Bank and Trust Commission--initial date is 1955 for expenditures, 1959 for size of regulated activity; Dept. of Insurance--initial date is 1958 for expenditures, 1959 for regulated activity; Dept. of Agriculture--initial date is 1958 for both series.

**
Generally gross receipts; number of aircraft for Aeronautics Com.; value of assets of Illinois banks for Bank and Trust Com.; number of nonagricultural employees for Department of Labor.

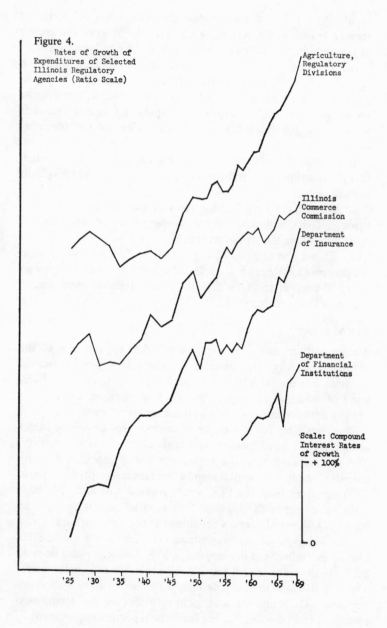

Figure 4.
Rates of Growth of
Expenditures of Selected
Illinois Regulatory
Agencies (Ratio Scale)

Agriculture,
Regulatory
Divisions

Illinois
Commerce
Commission

Department
of Insurance

Department
of Financial
Institutions

Scale: Compound
Interest Rates
of Growth
⌐ + 100%

∟ 0

'25 '30 '35 '40 '45 '50 '55 '60 '65 '69

regulatory activities share two characteristics, however: persistent secular growth and a very loose relationship between the growth of the regulated activity and the growth of the regulatory agency.

All the expenditure data in this section are reported in current dollars and in this inflation-ridden age it is necessary to pay at least passing attention to the deflated expenditures. There exists no accepted price index of the cost of operating regulatory bodies so we have constructed a very crude index by the following procedure:

1. Assume that all expenditures are for personnel. In actual fact the fraction of expenditures on personnel is about four-fifths in most agencies.[13]

2. Average the Civil Service rates of pay for the ranks G-8 through G-10, within which the average rank of personnel of most federal regulatory agencies fall.

The deflated and undeflated expenditures of all federal agencies are presented in figure 5. Undeflated expenditures of all agencies rose 550 percent from 1945 to 1967, but deflated expenditures rose only 150 percent.

FEE SYSTEMS

Almost without exception regulatory bodies require fees of the regulated activity: the three main exceptions among federal agencies are the NLRB, the Antitrust Division, and the FTC, none of which deals regularly with any given industry.[14] We explore here certain attributes of these fee structures.

The regulatory fee is a major instrument for acquiring information on the locus, parties, and scale of the regulated activity. The parties subject to the regulatory policy are identified by periodic fees as an essential step in the regulatory process. Some 1970 examples from the FCC are:[15] Annual AM and FM radio stations: 24 times the highest "one-minute" spot rates (but at least $52). Renewal licenses for subscriber stations in rural radio service, $25. Application to construct land line coaxial cable, $100 plus $5 per mile. Ship license, radio, $25. Amateur radio license, $9. Virtually every agency which deals regularly and continuously with a particular industry or occupation joins a fee system to licenses.[16] Governments and nonprofit bodies are frequently exempted from the fees but not from the reporting requirement.

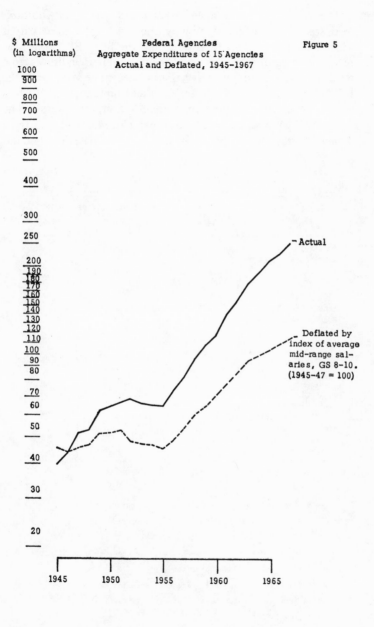

$ Millions
(in logarithms)

Federal Agencies
Aggregate Expenditures of 15 Agencies
Actual and Deflated, 1945-1967

Figure 5

Actual

Deflated by
index of average
mid-range sal-
aries, GS 8-10.
(1945-47 = 100)

The variation among agencies in the share of expenditures recovered from fees levied directly upon the regulated activity is wide (see table 4). Only three agencies, the FCC, FPC, and SEC recover any significant fraction of their annual expenditures from fees. In large measure, however, this is a deceptive arithmetic: the FCC's fees do not include the taxes on telephones, nor do the fees of the ICC include the taxes on transportation, for example. The industry which is so powerful that it can obtain large boons from the government will also, if it provides the lucrative demand

TABLE 4

FEE REVENUES OF FEDERAL AGENCIES

AGENCY	Ratio,Fees to Expenditures 1969*	ANNUAL RATE OF GROWTH, 1950-69*	
		Expenditures	Fees
Antitrust	0	5.4%	0
Civil Aeronautics Bd.	.094[a]	8.2	b
FCC	.229	6.9	c
ICC	.044[d]	6.4[e]	17.6%[e]
FTC	.003[f]	8.9	20.0[f]
Food & Drug Admin.	.051	16.2	7.1
Federal Home Loan Bank	g	13.1	g
FPC	.522[h]	8.4	10.3[h]
NLRB	0	8.7	0
SEC	1.185	7.7	13.7
Comm. Exchange Author.	.022	5.1	4.9
Wage and Hour Division	0	7.9	0
Tariff Commission	0	6.9	0
Maritime Comm.	.008	8.4[i]	-3.1[i]
Packer and Stock- yards Admin.	0	9.6	0

*Unless otherwise specified.

[a]1968 ratio.

[b]Begins 1968, hence growth rate not computed.

[c]Begins 1965, hence growth rate not computed.

[d]1967 ratio--see e.

[e]1950-67; 1967 is latest year available comparable with 1950.

[f]"Fees" include fines, penalties, etc.

[g]Primarily self-supporting agency, assessing members.

[h]Includes head-water benefit payments in fees.

[i]Begins 1963.

conditions, be heavily taxed: thus in 1968 the petroleum industry received benefits of $3 billion or more under the oil import quota system, but collected $3 billion in gasoline taxes for the federal treasury (and $5 billion for state governments). The motor trucking industry received partial protection from competition through the ICC—for which no value has been estimated—but paid special taxes of $4.7 billion (primarily to states) in the same year.

The simultaneous granting of regulatory benefits and levying of taxes poses an obvious question: if the industry has sufficient political power to obtain a state-supported cartel, why cannot the industry avoid becoming the object of selective excise taxation? This is clearly a question that fits the domestic petroleum industries of extraction and refining, the telephone industry, the trucking industry, and several other recipients of regulatory benefits. Several possible answers may be given:

1. The tax revenues are used for the benefit of the regulated industry. For example, the revenue from taxes on gasoline is often pledged to highway construction. This explanation fails on two counts. First, some industry tax revenues are not systematically so earmarked (SEC, liquor taxes), and second, even with the dedication of revenues the industry would be better off if these costs were imposed upon the general fund.[17]

2. More valuable regulatory services are provided to some industries than to others, and corresponding charges are made of the industry. Casual impressions are not cordial to the hypothesis: the FCC protection against new rivals has been extremely valuable, but television and radio franchises are not heavily taxed; the special beneficiaries of the farm price support programs have not been taxed in proportion to benefits (sugar and cotton are not taxed, tobacco is heavily taxed, etc.). We should expect an electoral majority capable of charging for benefits to be capable of withholding the benefits when the payments are small.

3. The dominant political coalition uses excises on the industry to redistribute income to itself. The necessary conditions for such a use of selective fees and taxes are two: the burden of the taxes should be borne by a widely diffused class (which therefore cannot organize to oppose the tax), and the elasticity of demand is small (so large revenues can be obtained).[18]

This last explanation is a special case of the obvious characteristic of democratic political life: special minorities (including industries) can exploit uninterested majorities but will be exploited by interested majorities.[19]

The Illinois state regulatory agencies are more commonly credited with the revenues of taxes, so the corresponding ratios of receipts to expenditures are often well in excess of unity (see table 5). In the more parsimonious halls of state houses, fees also systematically grow at least as rapidly as regulatory expenditures.[20]

TABLE 5

ILLINOIS REGULATORY AGENCIES, TRENDS OF EXPENDITURES AND FEES, 1950-68

AGENCY	Ratio,Fees to Expenditures 1968*	ANNUAL RATE OF GROWTH, 1950-68*	
		Expenditures	Fees
Aeronautics Comm.	0.09	8.1%	9.4%
Bank & Trust Comm.	0.81	3.4	20.7
Commerce Comm.	1.14[a]	3.7	13.4[a]
Dept. of Financial Institutions	0.61	4.3[b]	14.2[b]
Dept. of Insurance	26.65[c]	4.6	5.9[c]
Liquor Control Comm.	2.10	1.8	-1.3
Mines & Minerals	0.08[d]	3.0[d]	0.7[d]
Securities Div. of Sec. of State	1.90	3.5[e]	7.6[e]
Dept. of Agriculture, Regulatory Divisions	.25	5.8	4.3
Dept. of Labor, Regulatory Divisions	0.10	2.3	3.6

*Unless another year is specified.

[a]Estimated. Includes Public Utility Gross Revenue Tax in fees.

[b]Initial year is 1959.

[c]Includes Privilege Tax in fees.

[d]1966 is latest year available.

[e]Initial year is 1958.

THE PERSONNEL OF REGULATION COMMISSIONS

Our theory of industry-acquired regulation predicts that the regulatory body will have the character of a trustworthy bureaucracy rather than the dangerous potentialities of competitive politics. The regulating agency must eventually become the agency of the regulated industry, if it has a well-defined area of responsibility. This is not to say that it will be bribed into corruption or even that relationships between agency and industry are always cordial. Yet each needs the other. No one else will appear each year before the appropriation committees of Congress to support the agency's requests for more powers and funds. Ida Tarbell may have been tenacious in her pursuit of Standard Oil of New Jersey, but no granddaughter of hers has made the annual pilgrimage to the Oil Import Quota office of the Department of the Interior and the Texas Railroad Commission. Conversely, the agency *could*, in the short run, impose large costs upon the regulated industry if it undertook hostile or heretical policies.

Such things cannot be left to chance, and the appointments to the regulatory commissions must avoid at least violent industry opposition and preferably obtain industry support. It is interesting to observe that no federal regulatory body (except the Federal Reserve Board) has an economist commissioner, or has had one in memory of living man—they will have stronger commitments to their university than to the regulated industry.[21] It is more interesting that no ambitious politician is provided a springboard: let us examine how extraordinarily conventional the regulators' careers are.

Consider first the study of commissioners of federal regulatory bodies made by E. Pendleton Herring. (*Federal Commissioners* [Cambridge, Mass.: Harvard University Press, 1936]).

Prior work: "Our data indicate the predominating professional and at times even professorial tone of this group." Of those with prior federal service, "our commissioners have been recruited chiefly from three sources: namely, from the ranks of those performing legislative, legalistic, or technical functions" (ibid., pp. 41, 50).

Age: "Only 21 men (out of 143) under the age of 45 have been appointed, while those ranging from 45 to 54 years of age reach a total of 68" (ibid., p. 58)—and those 55 and over number 54. .

Subsequent   Of the 75 commissioners who had left office and
Public   were still active (42 still serving and 26 dead,
Service: retired, or unknown), 3 were subsequently *elected* to
              Congress or Senate. Twenty-nine held appointive
              offices, 25 were in legal practice and 14 in business
              (ibid., pp. 133, 135).[22]

The commissioners are of an age, background, and prospects
such that they are not likely to benefit by a major controversy with
the regulated industry. They are more likely to have retired from
elective politics than to be entering it.[23]

   A more recent investigation of the commissioners in two
regulatory commissions, the FTC and the SEC, is presented in
table 6. Again we find that overwhelmingly the commissioners are
either executives or lawyers, hardly ever entering elective political

TABLE 6

PROFILE OF SEC AND FTC
COMMISSIONERS THROUGH 1968

	SEC	FTC
Number of Commissioners	43	40
Average age at appointment	45.9	49.7
A. Distribution of years from education to appointment:		
1. Legal practice, private	33.5%	33.2%
2. Elective office	3.3%	15.5%
3. Other government office	36.3%	36.8%
(of which regulatory agencies =)	(19.3%)	(14.9%)
4. Business	21.4%	11.4%
5. Academic	5.6%	3.0%
Number for which above information available	43	39
Average term in office completed	3.7 yrs.	6.0 yrs.
Number of past Commissioners	39	35
B. Distribution of years from leaving commission to retirement or death:		
1. Legal practice, private	29.6&	55.0%
2. Elective office	1.0%	8.8%
3. Other government office	29.7%	20.7%
(of which regulatory agencies =)	(1.2%)	(5.3%)
4. Business	36.5%	11.4%
5. Academic	3.2%	4.0%
Number for which above information available	38	34

life. The commissioners wish to pursue the occupation of honored executive. The careers of the bureau chiefs of these agencies are, if possible, even more committed to public non-elective service (table 7).

TABLE 7

PROFILE OF SEC AND FTC
BUREAU CHIEFS, 1948 THROUGH 1968

	SEC	FTC
Number of Bureau Chiefs	24	16
Average at appointment	40.5	54.0
A. Distribution of years from education to appointment:		
1. Legal practice, private	32.3%	7.4%
2. Elective office	0.0%	0.0%
3. Other government office (of which regulatory agencies =)	63.8%	79.9%
	(54.2%)	(73.8%)
4. Business	3.9%	3.7%
5. Academic	0.0%	9.0%
Number for which above information available	10	9
Average term in office completed	3.7 yrs.[a]	4.1 yrs.[a]
Number of past Bureau Chiefs	20	10
B. Distribution of years from leaving position to retirement or death:		
1. Legal practice, private	50.0%	35.7%
2. Elective office	0.0%	0.0%
3. Other government office (of which regulatory agencies =)	25.7%	14.3%
	(24.3%)	(14.3%)
4. Business	4.3%	0.0%
5. Academic	20.0%	50.0%
Number for which above information available	10	3

[a]Average term in office for past bureau chiefs with biographical information = SEC - 4.1; FTC - 5.0.

The regulator who seeks to maximize his utility subject to continuance in office—or related political or industry work thereafter—must avoid open conflicts with the regulated industry. A regulator must have cooperation in achieving either the appearance or the substance of any regulatory goals. He might make political capital out of a pitched battle with the industry, but that capital would be valuable to a man seeking public elective office, not to a career-minded regulator. The industry can be helpful at every turn: for example, one utility executive related how rate reductions desired by his company are effected by informing the regulatory commission, which then received due credit for ordering the universally desired reduction. The regulator reciprocates by supporting those policies—above all, control over entry—which contribute to the "stability" and "responsibility" of the industry.[24]

A few regulatory bodies are not confined to one or a few industries, occupations, or other organized groups: the Antitrust Division is the classical example, now being joined by a variety of consumer protective bodies. On our theory of industry-regulatory body marriage, these general purpose agencies will be less "bureaucratic" in their staffing, less cartel-minded in their economic policies—and harder put to maintain their appropriations.

10

Regulation:
The Confusion of
Means and Ends

There is widespread agreement on the regulation of economic and social affairs in the United States. The subject is a relatively uncontroversial one.

Public regulation is relatively uncontroversial in an ideological sense: there are only a few people who go to the extremes which surround current policy. A few people, indeed, believe that almost all regulation is bad, and by a singular coincidence a significant fraction of the academic part of this group resides within a radius of one mile of my university. Somewhat more people believe that regulation is wholly insufficient or inefficient, and that the explicit vesting of much privately owned enterprise in direct governmental ownership and operation is essential to satisfactory social performance. These old-fashioned socialists have always had some trouble discussing the post office; when the sovereign cannot carry small rectangular pieces of paper with either economy or dispatch, one must inevitably worry about his capacity to manage an entire economy. Recently the socialists have been dealt a fierce and unscrupulous blow, the nationalization of passenger train service.

The great majority of Americans would not dream of abandoning the important regulatory policies, and are in full agreement with a regime which adds five or ten new regulatory items a year. As recently as October 21 of this year [1972] this majority had the good fortune to obtain a law authorizing the Secretary of Transportation to order heavier bumpers for automobiles and to jail men found tampering with the mileage on an odometer. We may confidently await new regulations of other parts of a motor vehicle, and of the thousand other ingredients of everyday living.

The regulatory policies are uncontroversial, accordingly, in a political sense. The major parties do not dispute their existence, and seldom their detailed policies. Each year the appropriations of each regulatory body grow about 8 percent on average: 1 percent for population, 5 percent for prices, and 2· percent for growing evil. The momentum of events is awesome.

Most basically, there is scarcely a murmur of controversy on the goals of social policy. Everyone wants a good deal of purity in goods and wholesomeness in environment; they want safety in automobiles and in financial institutions; they want reliable service in airlines, competence in doctors, erudition or at least incomprehensibility in professors, and sunshine on weekends. Everyone wants poverty eliminated, families united—no matter what the cost in psychiatric care—and crime abated, or at least confined to certain localities.

To be sure, a list of good things will seldom create controversy if each person is allowed his own priorities, or, differently put, if the price tags are not attached. In fact, there is no substantive difference between hating a thing and professing love for it if only the price were not undeniably exorbitant. And with our opulent nation and our rapidly growing public sector, publicly supplied good things seem hardly to confront a problem of scarcity: almost every old and new program can be and in fact has been increasing rapidly.

In this connection, a special word of praise is due to Professor Galbraith, the leading spokesman for the underpriviliged public sector. As of the recent past and present time his message was of course absurd. The non-defense budget of our nation—state and local as well as federal governments—has been growing at the rate of 10 percent per year since 1960. The public sector has been starved for only one thing: remotely promising enterprises on which to spend money. But in another decade that picture will change radically, and no doubt that prospective picture was what Galbraith had or should have had in mind. The aggregate expansion of the public sector will slow down rapidly, and the theory of opportunity cost will return from exile to full residence in Washington and the state capitals. Granting that scarcity eventually intrudes on all of men's activities, however, up to now we have been spared the harsh controversies of difficult public choices.

One may distinguish two kinds of public regulations, and I wish to discuss the problems of enforcement of regulation of only one kind. The kind of regulation I propose to ignore is industry-oriented and almost invariably industry-dominated: the various petroleum programs, the regulation of transportation and communication industries, and the like. Regulations in these industries are directed primarily to industry benefits, and the industry usually plays a large role in their enforcement [see chap. 8 of this volume].

The second kind of regulation is general purpose: the collection of a general income tax; the control of monopoly wherever it arises (antitrust policy); the protection of consumers against fraud and defective products. The distinction between this kind of regulation and industry regulation is not unambiguous: the Food and Drug Administration is directed to a few industries and is part of a program of general protection of consumers. Yet the distinction is useful, and I propose to discuss in the remainder of this paper the problems of efficient enforcement of these general economic policies. The laws with any and all of their blemishes will be accepted as goals, but reconsidered as instruments to achieve these goals.

What is not commonly realized is that there are several ways to skin even a reforming cat. The traditional, not to say unthinking, reliance upon the appointment of a regulatory body is not the only, or even often a reasonable, method of advancing our regulatory goals. To tell an agency to go out and see that others sin no more is not to solve a problem except in the important sense of getting it off the agenda for the time being. One must ask of every regulatory agent

—is he qualified?

—is he given proper incentives?

—is there an audit of his performance?

—and, is it possible to challenge failures or weaknesses in his performance?

I propose to submit our regulatory agencies to these tests. I shall make extensive use of an article by Gary Becker and myself on the enforcement of rules ("Law Enforcement, Malfeasance, and Compensation of Enforcers," *Journal of Legal Studies* 3 [January 1974]: 1–18).

ARE REGULATORS QUALIFIED?

I assert that regulators are or can be fully qualified. If the state wishes, it can employ skilled men with specialized knowledge, it can persuade them to be diligent, and it can achieve good levels of integrity. Of course, it can fail in all these respects, but so too can profit-making institutions. If the state wishes to pay the market rate, it can hire men of high ability.

Thus I reject the popular view that bureaucrats are inherently incompetent or lazy or timid in the conduct of public affairs. This view is often based simply upon ancient prejudice, but it is sometimes supported by the argument that in a non-profit-making organization there are no definite measures of and incentives to efficient performance. I postpone that issue, and simply reaffirm that the state can and does hire able people, whether they use their ability properly or not.

General ability is not the whole content of a qualified person, however. Consider the enforcement of the Sherman Act. Presently it is enforced by a troop of lawyers, aided by some FBI agents and occasionally a stray economist—all, let us assume, of the highest quality. How can this collection of people, removed from commerce and largely concentrated in the nation's capital, know whether company W in industry X is violating the Act in state Y with respect to commodity Z? The only way in which the Antitrust Division could possibly learn of this violation is if it received a letter of complaint from an aggrieved party. Many such letters are received, but there is surely no serious presumption that the most serious violations call forth the first and the most helpful complaints—that would be fortuitous in the extreme.

Or consider the determination whether a given product is produced under sanitary conditions. The probability of a violation depends upon the production process, the raw materials, the quality of labor, and similar factors known primarily to the industry and its suppliers and customers. These circumstances change frequently and vary widely from plant to plant, even from one manager to the next, and from one shift of operations to the next. Even an experienced corps of inspectors will be less skilled than the people directly concerned with the industry in detecting violations.

The argument can be generalized: very seldom, indeed, will the regulators be well situated in experience and knowledge to detect and prove violations. A dozen people are more likely than the IRS to know whether X is cheating on his tax, and a score of truckers know better than the ICC whether firm Y is violating its certificate restrictions. Professional competence and integrity are not sufficient to qualify one as a superior enforcer.

THE INCENTIVES OF REGULATORS

A rational man must be guided by the incentive system within which he operates. No matter what his own personal desires, he must be discouraged from certain activities if they carry penalties and attracted toward others if they carry large rewards. The carrot and the stick guide scientists and politicians as well as donkeys.

An efficient enforcement system, therefore, requires intelligent guides to the regulators, telling them which things are good and also important, which ones are good but unimportant, and which are positively harmful. All too often the system of values, or incentives, is badly skewed. This is a fault, not of the regulators, but of the legislatures and executives who establish the incentives. Let me give three examples.

First, very often the regulators proudly tell us how many cases they have won: how many adulterators they have apprehended, how may false advertisements they have challenged, how many thieves they have jailed. This is as if General Electric told us proudly how many items it had produced last year, counting aircraft engines equally with turbines and refrigerators and light bulbs. Such a report would properly cause General Electric to be ridiculed, but each year the FTC gravely reports the number of cease and desist orders it has mailed out. We should demand measures of performance which take account of importance.

Second, failures are not free to regulators, but they are seldom charged the full cost. If a violation is improperly charged, and the party is acquitted, he is reimbursed neither for the costs of his defense nor for the damage done to his reputation. This tyrannical vestige of the age of absolute sovereigns is so indefensible that it is impossible for me to conceive of a defense sufficiently respectable to deserve examination. I should think that, at a very minimum, the regulatory agency should be required to reimburse direct expenses after every acquittal and insert a quarter-page ad in 10 national newspapers and magazines withdrawing all accusations with apology. This practice should, of course, be associated with an increase in agency appropriations: the purpose of the scheme is to place the cost of error on the society rather than on the victim. Error is inevitable, but regulators should be given incentives to minimize it.

There is yet another kind of regulatory failure: nonfeasance. To act slowly (which has one special but non-empty subcategory, "taking forever to act") often has no easily identifiable costs to society. If the FCC takes interminable ages to allow the introduction of pay-TV, only one or two pioneer companies seem to be mildly injured. In fact, of course, a thousand firms have been denied existence, and you and I have been denied programs for which I would have been an eager purchaser for half a generation. The suppression of this boon to minority audiences has surely done me more harm than all the other actions of the FCC have ever done me good. Sam Peltzman's study of the cost of the FDA's restriction and delay of new drugs ("An Evaluation of Consumer Protection Legislation: The 1962 Drug Amendments," *Journal of Political Economy* 81, no. 5 [Sept.-Oct. 1973]: 1049-91) is both pathbreaking and monumental, and I look forward confidently to the expansion of our knowledge of these costs of nonfeasance in regulation as other scholars follow his example and methods.

Unlike the problem of charging innocent people, the problem of delay has no simple solution. Regulation is an activity of human beings in a complex and imperfectly understood world, so regulators—like brides, musicians, and professors—are entitled to some mistakes, or rather, cannot possibly avoid all mistakes. There are almost no effective sanctions upon delay if the consent of the regulator is necessary: even if the regulatory body is given a short period within which to act (as is true, for example, of SEC review of new prospectuses), the agency has such large discretionary powers in asking for further information or otherwise burdening an enterprise as to rob the time limit of content. Unless the controversial behavior may continue until stopped by the regulator, a time limit should be an element of every statute, although a uniform time limit is a crude tool to shape a variegated world. A better remedy for delay will be proposed later.

The first problem of regulation, the lack of guides to the selection of important cases, does allow of substantial correction even with our present regulatory procedures. The penalties for violations of statues should be proportioned to the harm which these violations impose on society. A technical violation which simply affronts the dignity of the regulatory body should call forth a small fine. A major violation should correspondingly incur a major fine. We should not specify the fines in statutes—saying, as the Sherman Act does, that a maximum offense will be fined $50,000, or, with the Copeland Act, that a second offense of food adulteration will have a maximum fine of $10,000. The fines should be proportioned to the severity of the harm done by the violation, and should be larger, the smaller the probability of dectection of the offense. Then the violator will face a rational system of deterrence, and the regulatory body will face a rational system of incentives and of measurement of performance.

AUDITING THE REGULATOR

The auditing of the performance of a regulatory body is now seldom undertaken by any responsible public body. A congressional committee may subject the routine operations of an agency to close, and possibly headline-oriented, review once every twenty or eighty years. The Office of Management and Budget will ask for some numbers of the kind I have just deplored. The main check on the agency comes from the industry or activity it regulates. That is where one finds the combination of strong and continuing financial interest and intensive knowledge—and of course the knowledge is a result of the financial interest—which guarantee close, informed scrutiny and vigorous legal and political action.

This is a splendid check, but of course it is a check against only certain types of error in regulation. Industry review will guarantee that the FDIC does not charter too many new banks (as if that were conceivable) or fail to close down those without charter. Industry review will guarantee that rates of domestic and international airlines do not become too cheap. But industry review will not combat the monopoly-creating propensities which inhere in virtually all regulation, and almost by definition it is inappropriate to the class of general regulatory policy which I am discussing.

The only non-industry audit that an agency must fear is that of the reformer, be he a professor or an evangelical lawyer. The professor is an easy burden: if he is responsible and competent, we can be certain that his audience will be at most in the hundreds, not in the hundreds of thousands or millions. The Nader type of reformer is more fearsome, because he is armed with passion, and any irresponsibility and slovenliness in his accusations seems to have little cost to him. But he is a feeble reed on which to rest the public welfare, and for two reasons. First, he lives on headlines, so he must flit from one sin to another, and for him one fresh $5 million scandal is worth $100 million of day-in, day-out routine inefficiency. Secondly, because he is untrained or half-trained, he has no real remedy for a regulatory failure except indignation, a new set of faces, and a stern admonition to sin no more. Consider what is basically a shallow, shoddy piece of work, the Cox-Fellmeth study of the FTC (Edward F. Cox, Robert C. Fellmeth, and John E. Schultz, *The Nader Report on the Federal Trade Commission* [New York: Grove Press, 1969]). They seek to strengthen some of the silliest activities of the commission, such as the regulation of advertising. They calmly ignore its nearly sixty years of history, and ask now for only five new faces! This sort of audit of regulation cries for regulation of auditors.

The appraisal of the achievements of a regulatory body is not impossible: a whole series of such appraisals is gradually developing an arsenal of techniques for measurement. I may cite the Coleman study of school segregation, the forthcoming New Jersey study of income maintenance plans, as well as a large number of economic studies, many of which have appeared in the *Journal of Law and Economics*. It would be at least a minor improvement of our world if once a decade each major regulator was reviewed by a committee appointed by the appropriate scientific body, with funds and subpoena powers provided by the OMB.

The Improvability of Regulation

Suppose a citizen becomes convinced that a particular regulatory agency is thoroughly remiss in its enforcement of a statutory policy. This is not a strenuous supposition: even the most exemplary regulatory body has its periods of inanimation or even of perversion of policy, and this period will sometimes be very long. The one recourse this citizen now has, aside from resignation, is to launch a crusade: to write to his congressman, who receives many letters, to his editor, who publishes few, and to what always proves to be so embarrassingly small, his public. Even a professor of economics is, as I observed in connection with the auditing function, a very small voice, for the excellent reason that there are so many professors that if each had a loud voice, the noise would be defeaning. There is no satisfactory recourse for the informed and diligent citizen when he encounters a regulatory failure.

Indeed the shield of invulnerability seems almost impenetrable to assaults even by substantial groups, let alone individual citizens. Consider the fixed commission structure of the New York Stock Exchange, which has dwelled under the shelter of SEC patronage and hence presumable exemption from the Sherman Act. Major changes brought about by major groups have resulted from this grievious malfeasance of the SEC: the third market has developed; the "give-ups" were developed to a high level; and institutional membership in the regional exchanges has begun. The SEC continued its bland neglect of the public interest in this area until a year ago, when negotiated rates were commanded where they are not needed—for very large transactions. The great mutual funds and pension funds and insurance companies could not bring about an appropriate, fully authorized SEC decision to instill competition in this price structure.

The present system does not allow small groups to operate effectively on the great stage of national regulation: one must launch a large political campaign or he must remain silent. This discontinuity, this permissible insularity of the regulatory bodies, no doubt has its merits: the agencies are not engaged in constant disputes, listening to fools and knaves as well as angels. But it builds an all-or-none element into regulatory reform.

A Modest Proposal

One of the greatest merits of the economic system is that it has learned to overcome precisely this problem. Suppose I wish a kind of textbook in economics different from all those now available. It is not necessary for me to convince a federal board of editors, or the congressional committee which controls it, to make a substantial shift in its publishing program. The very size of such a board, and the very diversity of interests of affected parties, would normally lead the board to file my suggestion in a paper shredder. No, now I can appeal to any one publisher, argue the commercial promise of the venture, and, if I can succeed in persuading a single publisher (or become one myself), my idea will be tried. If I am wholly correct in my view of what the market wishes, a herd of publishers will then follow my successful (meaning profitable) leadership.

This suggests, and I now wish explicitly to propose, the introduction of competition into the enforcement of regulation. Our survey of the problems of enforcement found four difficulties with the system of enforcement by a specialized regulatory service:

1. The public agents, even though trained and diligent, are often very poorly situated to discover violations, and never *better* situated than all other groups in the society.

2. The incentives to regulators to concentrate on larger problems, and to speed, are weak because legislatures have not been persuaded to strengthen them. Improved legislation may provide guidance on the importance of cases, but it does not seem possible to devise an efficient incentive to speed.

3. The auditing of regulatory agencies requires a continuous expenditure of substantial resources, and only one group in the society—those primarily subject to the regulations—have the incentive to provide these resources.

4. If a regulatory agency performs badly, there is no recourse open to individuals or small groups.

All of these difficulties except the provision of proper incentives will be resolved if any person who wishes is allowed to enforce regulatory statutes. In particular,

1. Those best informed about violations will be enlisted to stop them.

2. Since enforcement will be a profitable undertaking for superior enforcers, we can expect diligence, dispatch and innovation. If fines are made proportional to the harm done by a violation, incentives to enforcement will be proportional to the demonstrated damage from violations, so enforcement efforts will be concentrated on the most damaging violations.

3. If public agencies also enforce statutes in competition with private parties, the auditing of both will be undertaken by

competitors in the process. If a public regulator overlooks large violations, private enforcers will find the area profitable.

4. Anyone who detects an enforcement failure can enter into the enterprise of enforcement.

Support for these propositions will be found in the paper by Becker and me mentioned earlier in this essay.

This proposal is not so radical as may appear. The triple damage suit has become much the most important sanction of the Sherman Act, and the lawyers specializing in this area are even preparing the evidence required to show violation of the statute. Class action legislation intended to codify and no doubt to limit this new type of enforcement will presumably be passed soon by Congress. The only deterrent I would put on class actions is the requirement that if defendants are acquitted, complete compensation of all costs be provided by the plaintiff. We have traditionally used private assistance extensively in public enforcement, although with such opprobrious titles as informers. Indeed the most popular lawyers' reaction to our proposal is that private competition will lead to too much enforcement!

Anyone who rejects this proposal, for good reasons or bad, ought to face squarely the question: how will he discharge the four main tasks of enforcement? How will he find the information, direct the regulators to the expeditious pursuit of major violators, assure himself of the continued reliability of the regulator, and bring about needed reforms? Public regulation, for all its enormous momentum, lives by its goals and not by its achievements, and surely we ought eventually to tire of promising preambles and unpromising achievement.

Can Regulatory
Agencies Protect
the Consumer?

The consumer—and the investor and the laborer—have always been subjected to vicissitudes arising out of chance, ignorance, neglect, and fraud. Some are essentially inescapable: no sovereign has discovered a way to insure that everything taught in school is correct. Some are largely avoidable, but sometimes at costs more onerous than the vicissitudes: consider how much time would be required thoroughly to test ten competing brands of a product. That may very well be the reason there is no business which supplies leading brands of goods for experiment by the prospective buyer.

For the long centuries during which the state concerned itself little with such problems, the consumer had two main resources in dealing with the possible vicissitudes of purchasing, lending, working, and living. The first resource was his own intelligence, enshrined in the doctrine of *caveat emptor*. That phrase poorly describes the situation, and for at least three reasons:

1. The consumer did not have to beware of everything: he could contract with the seller for express warranties with respect to the commodity, and these warranties were and are enforceable.

2. There were implied warranties that the goods were of merchantable quality: the seller was required to reveal defects which would not be discoverable with ordinary examination.

3. The seller then, as now, had a good deal to beware of too. Anyone who thinks that there are more careless, irresponsible, or dishonest sellers than buyers obviously has never been a seller.

There was a second resource of the consumer to deploy against the vicissitudes of inferior performance, and that was the great engine of competition. It is widely assumed that if company A produces shoddy goods, rival B must also lower the quality of its goods to compete in price. That is exactly the opposite of the

This essay was presented in a debate with Manuel Cohen; the full exchange is in *Can Regulatory Agencies Protect the Consumer?* (American Enterprise Institute, 1971).

typical sequence: it is usually profitable to compete by improving quality, reliability, and safety. Consider just two types of evidence for the protective function of competition:

1. It is commonplace that there has been a strong secular trend in the improvement of the quality of manufactured goods. Tires last longer and seldom blow out; food is cleaner; antibiotics are more effective. To quote the National Bureau of Economic Research's Committee on Price Statistics:

> If a poll were taken by professional economists and statisticians they would designate (and by a wide majority) the failure of the price indexes to take full account of quality changes as the most important defect in these indexes. And by almost as large a majority, they would believe that this failure introduces a systematic upward bias in the price indexes—that quality changes on average have been quality improvements.[1]

2. The great merchandising dynasties—the Marshall Fields, the Macys, the Lazarus companies, Sears Roebuck, and Ward—are famous for their standards of reliability, not for the skill with which they ignore a customer's complaints. Their main asset, and the source of their economic prosperity, is their reputation for fair and careful dealing. Similarly with manufacturers: Henry Ford became enormously richer than Lydia Pinkham.

Of course, neither the diligence of ordinary mortals nor the competitive energies of an extraordinary economy will detect and prevent or correct all the mishaps and negligences and frauds of life. In Barnum's time a sucker may have been born every minute: now the population is three times as big and surely even (or especially?) in America at least several rogues are born every hour. So it is natural to turn to that center of authority, that depository of virtue and benevolence, that fountain of justice, the state, to provide further and fuller protection to the consumer. We are now well launched upon a luxuriously prolific regime of laws and agencies to protect the consumer. Any underestimate which the state may have made in the past of the need for protecting the individual in economic (and social) life is being more than corrected by the vigor and extravagance of its belated efforts.

The question before the house is what the government can do to help the consumer. Discussion of this question can proceed at either of two levels.

The first, and overwhelmingly popular, level of discourse is deductive and horatory. Appoint to a commission seven highly intelligent men who have unflagging zeal to serve the public interest, and only the public interest, equip them with the resources to find out what to do, and give them the legal power to do it. Then automobiles will be safe, stock exchanges will charge reasonable commissions, and mutual funds will not spend too much on selling costs. If on occasion a commissioner is less than superb, replace him; if on occasion the commission does something wrong, reprimand it; if the commission does too little, enlarge its powers and fatten its appropriations. With at most an occasional searching glance from the legislature, the agency will take care of monopolistic railroads, or profit-grubbing television, or deceptively quoted interest rates, or whatever. In this easy world we would need only listen to the demands of a Mr. Ralph Nader each day and fashion a new agency to solve his problem: one agency = one problem solved. The only suitable word to terminate such a discussion is "Amen": have not five or seven apostles been dealt off the top?

There is a second level of discourse, and I shall be so stubborn as to refuse to leave it during the remainder of this paper. It proceeds rather differently. The state has been protecting consumers for quite a time: for example, it is eighty-three years [1971] since the Interstate Commerce Commission (ICC) was created to assure safety of trains, adequacy of service, and reasonableness of rates. For fifty-six years the Federal Trade Commission (FTC) has been stamping out unfair methods of competition; for sixty-four years food and drug products have been under federal control; and even the Securities and Exchange Commission (SEC) is thirty-six years old, and no longer able to sprint. The vast body of actual experience, not the prospectuses of reformers, must be the basis upon which we appraise the role of the government in protecting the consumer.

If commissioners have often been lazy or timid, or deeply subservient to the industry they purport to regulate, it is inexcusably romantic to assume that all future appointments will be regulatory saints. If, whatever the quality of commissioners, quite often the law dictates inherently anticonsumer policies, what purpose is there in unctuously demanding better laws from better Congresses? Or perhaps we should have a commission to regulate Congress? The regulatory experience is now sufficiently varied and lengthy so that we can isolate the essential characteristics of the regulatory process, characteristics which determine what, in fact, the consumer may expect from regulation.

I shall illustrate much of the subsequent discussion from the regulation of the security markets, but this is simply quixotic chivalry in meeting Mr. Cohen on his own field. Whatever the regulatory area of special interest, let me emphasize that our task is to ascertain the basic character of public regulation, not its incidental scandals or triumphs. I shall assume, what I believe to be true, that usually the regulators are honest and conscientious, and that in particular the SEC's members, and especially its past chairmen, are paragons of virtue. Our concern is with the logic and basic forces of regulation, and they not only transcend fluctuations in personnel and events but basically dictate what type of men (or rather, of that subset of men called lawyers) will typically be appointed.

And now to the main thesis: public regulation weakens the defenses the consumer has in the market and often imposes new burdens upon him, without confering corresponding protections. The doctrine of *caveat emptor* has not lost its force: the only change is that now the consumer must beware of different threats, and threats which he is less well equipped to defend against. The thesis will be developed with special reference to the SEC and the security markets.

We start with four important examples of the impairment of traditional consumer defenses by the SEC (acting often in collaboration with the New York Stock Exchange):

1. The New York Stock Exchange (NYSE) has imposed and enforced a minimum commission structure which is highly discriminatory against higher-priced stocks and larger-volume transactions and against nonmember brokers. No economist believes that it costs brokers ten times as much to sell 1,000 shares as 100 shares, or that a share selling for $100 costs substantially more to handle than one selling for $25, or that it is economically desirable that nonmember brokers share the work but not the

commission. This discriminatory structure of commissions has been set with the tacit and more recently explicit approval of the SEC, and this approval is the only defense of this flagrant cartel-determined price structure against attack under the anti-trust laws.

2. In the sale of mutual fund shares, the costs of the intial sale are much higher than the costs of collecting subsequent payments, and the mutuals have accordingly made a larger charge against the first-year contributions of a customer than against contributions in later years—a practice called "front-end loading." The SEC has now obtained legislation controlling front-end loading. Now the buyers of a mutual fund who do *not* withdraw from the fund will be permitted to bear the fund's costs in dealing with buyers who soon withdraw and are not charged the full costs of their temporary participation—a perverse incentive structure which must increase withdrawals. One could also raise some question of the equity of taxing the prudent to subsidize the impetuous. This SEC position stems from economic error, not industry pressure (as in the case of the commission structure).

3. Again, in the sale of mutual fund shares, a statutory provision (section 22 [d] of the Investment Company Act) compels all sellers of the shares to observe the offering price—a special and unusually rigid instance of resale price maintenance. The SEC explicitly refrained from requesting repeal of this extreme form of price-fixing by private enterprises.

4. The SEC has obtained legislation to regulate the selling expenses of mutual funds. The regulation of rates is of course a traditional regulatory weapon to defend the consumer, and in the case of railroad passengers has achieved almost 100 percent protection against both accidents and service. The SEC ceilings will make it more difficult for new funds to be launched and thus will reduce the competition which is the investor's main defense against excessive costs. The large, established mutual funds are naturally agreeable to this legislation.

These are examples of policies inimical to the investor's welfare which have been instituted or supported by the regulatory agency charged with protecting the investor. One could cite instances of nonfeasance as well: perhaps the most contemporary has been the practice of stock brokerage houses of operating on miserly capital bases, so that a moderate break in the market has led to a large number of failures. The SEC and its ally, the NYSE, have effectively delayed the brokerage houses which sought to go public and acquire an adequate volume of permanent capital not subject to partnership withdrawals—but I must add that most individual investors presumably are not so naive as to believe that the SEC's extensive regulation of this industry has increased the safety of its enterprises.

Competition, like other therapeutic forms of hardship, is by wide and age-long consent, highly beneficial to society when imposed upon—other people. Every industry that can afford a spokesman has emphasized both its devotion to the general principle and the overriding need for reducing competition within its own markets because this is the one area in which competition works poorly. The doctors must protect their patients against (unlicensed) quacks, and the medical profession must be right because Heaven has rewarded its benevolence with the highest earnings of any profession. Farmers must protect the consumer against famine, and this is best done by the subtle path of restrictions upon output and subsidies to producers.

Regulatory bodies are remarkably loyal in their acceptance of this two-edged philosophy—as indeed they should be, since they owe their existence to it. There may be instances in which the SEC, for example, has actually fostered competition in the industries for which it must answer to God, if not to man, and I hope that Mr. Cohen with his unrivaled knowledge can produce at least one. For every (or any) genuine instance that may be supplied, however, it will be ridiculously easy to supply five instances of the suppression of competition. Regulation and competition are rhetorical friends and deadly enemies: over the doorway of every regulatory agency save two should be carved: "Competition Not Admitted." The Federal Trade Commission's doorway should announce, "Competition Admitted in Rear," and that of the Antitrust Division, "Monopoly Only by Appointment."

Against the charge that public regulation imposes large costs, particularly by suppressing competition, the friends of public regulation will make three answers:

1. Some of the neglects—such as the monopolistic setting of commission rates and the inadequate capital requirements for stock exchange members—are about to be mended. One must make two decisive criticisms of this reply: (1) if evils persist for thirty-six years before they are mended, this is a grave criticism of the regulatory process; and (2) there is not the slightest assurance that the forthcoming reforms, if indeed they come forth, will remedy the past deficiencies. What historical justification is there for reverting to the theological level of discourse?

2. Some of the evils of the industry—such as the minimum commission on mutual fund share sales—are set by statute and hence are beyond the reach of the regulators. Observe: the effects of a regulation are to be judged not by the statutes actually passed by legislatures, but by those the friends of regulation would wish to see enacted.

3. There have been offsetting benefits of regulation, so that even if for argument's sake the complaints were accepted, the net balance would still be with regulation.

This third response is of course the crucial one, and it invites more extensive comment.

I am not prepared either to deny or to accept the proposition that the SEC has accomplished much good along with whatever harm to the investor it has fostered or supported. Like every other regulatory body, it has been virtually free of any objective measure of its economic effects, and indeed *effects* are seldom considered explicitly in its statements. For example, some years ago it won a case against an advisory service which bought and sold stocks prior to advising its subscribers to do the same. Did the SEC ask whether the subscribers were injured by the practice? Certainly not, for its concern was only with legalistic concepts of conflict of interest and economic substance was irrelevant. In fact, the subscribers to the service would have profited if they had followed, with a lag, the advice of the service (see table 1 in the notes to this chapter).[2]

Yet one test of the achievements of regulation in this area can be cited. Six years ago I made a study of the effects of the SEC's review of the prospectuses for new stock issues [chap. 6]. The procedure consisted basically of two steps:

1. A thousand dollars was hypothetically invested in each new

issue of common stock (above a certain minimum issue size) from 1923 to 1927 and from 1949 to 1955—thus before and after the SEC began to review prospectuses to ensure a measure of accurate information.

2. The performance in each case was compared with the movement of the stock market, as measured by the comprehensive Standard and Poor Index, in the same period.

The main finding was that in both periods the purchaser of new stock issues lost about 11 percent after one year and 21 percent after two years relative to buying the Standard and Poor stocks (see table 2 in the notes to this chapter).[3] One cannot claim utter precision for such a finding, but my conclusion is surely conservative: the SEC did not appreciably improve the experience of investors in the new issues market by its expensive review of prospectuses.

The record of regulation of the securities markets is wholly typical of regulatory programs. Consider the regulation of transportation. What does the consumer owe to the ICC? He owes for certain only two things: the support of a compulsory noncompetitive rate structure in the motor trucking industry, which, if not regulated, would be a highly competitive industry, and the imposition of a nonviable rigidity upon the railroad industry which is helping to destroy it before our eyes. What does the consumer owe the Civil Aeronautics Board (CAB)? Again, as with the ICC, very high barriers to the entry of new firms, and the support of a rate structure seriously in conflict with competition. What does the consumer owe to the regulation of television? Mainly such things as an extraordinary campaign to prevent and hamper pay television—although the main channel of this obstructive influence by commercial TV and movie theatre industries has been through the Congress, acting upon the Federal Communications Commission (FCC).

I have neither inclination nor evidence to deny the regulatory process occasional triumphs. The delay in introducing thalidomide in the United States presumably was a splendid success, and should receive full credit. But we must base public policy not upon signal triumphs or scandalous failures but upon the regular, average performance of the policy. If the policies which delayed thalidomide would delay a new penicillin at least as long—as seems highly probable—we must reckon this in the costs of the program.[4]

The ultimate, inescapable fact of life for the consumer is that he must beware—as much today as in the past. I began by saying that, under the earlier regime of *caveat emptor*, the consumer was protected basically by his own care and intelligence and by the most powerful of allies, competition. Public regulation weakens and sometimes destroys these defenses against fraud and negligence, without replacing the protections they used to afford.

Consider a regulatory activity—perhaps the federal milk marketing boards which have so carefully cartelized the production and distribution of milk in the United States, to the substantial economic detriment of the consumer. If one milk company exploits or misleads its customers, each consumer has an incentive to seek out a more reliable or more efficient supplier. The larger the misdeeds of this company, and the larger the consumption of milk by the consumer, the greater his rewards if he can uncover a new source of supply. Profit-seeking outsiders will strive mightily to respond to this demand for lower but profitable prices. These incentives provide a strong sanction even on a monopolist. (There is a widespread view that a monopolist profits by lowering the quality of goods compared to what competition would provide, and this view is simply erroneous economic theory. There is an equally popular view—often held by the very same people!—that competition leads to continuous reductions of quality and it is equally erroneous.)

What is the consumer's recourse if he is being exploited by a federal marketing order which either neglects his interests or, as is the case at present in the United States, positively arms and protects a cartel in exploiting this consumer? His sole defense is to organize a political campaign to change or eliminate that marketing scheme. For the individual consumer this is a bleak prospect. The costs—in time, effort, and money—to change legislation are large; the reward to any one consumer from joining a consumer lobby is negligible. The milk marketing board in Chicago, according to a competent economist's analysis, raised the price of milk at least two cents per quart in the mid-1960s—or perhaps $10 to $20 per family per year.[5] If a family were to devote a sum such as this to stirring up opposition to the marketing order, and even if the battle could be restricted to Chicago (the underlying legislation is federal), it would be a wretched option: the family would receive negligible benefits from its own activity.

The sheltered farmers, milk companies, and laborers in the industry have much larger stakes, and they can and do mount the legislative drives which create and dominate such legislation. The individual consumer has no real defense, given the nature of our political process, which allows compact groups with substantial per capita interests to win out over diffused masses of consumers, no one of whom can effectively combat special interest legislation.

Occasionally the consumer will be protected in the legislature by another industry which happens to share the consumer's goal but not his impotence. This fortuitous and uncommon circumstance aside, he is the victim without recourse of our political system which is inaccessible to groups that may be large but whose members as individuals have only small stakes in a controversy.

We are now going through a new period of salvation by public reform, similar in scale, and in the comparative roles assigned to emotion and to knowledge, to the muckraking period preceding World War I. Then we had Upton Sinclair and Ida Tarbell and a host of others; now we have Ralph Nader and his graduate and prep school students. In both periods the intellectual quality of the reform literature is, on all except its very best pages, rankly deplorable. Allegations are facts, villainy is ubiquitous, costs of reforms are not the rational prices which keep a sensible society from going overboard in one direction but the shallow, cynical excuses of the vested interests, and the federal political and administrative machinery is easily perfected in motive and achievement, once we replace the louts who have distorted and perverted it for many years! Even in the superior examples of this literature, such as the so-called Nader report (by Robert Fellmeth) on the Interstate Commerce Commission,[6] utter disillusionment with past regulation leads to a demand for better regulation! On this wave of sentiment, no doubt, a few pieces of reform—bad and good—will be brought in, but they will not amount to much.

They will not amount to much because there is no durable, effective political basis to support—or direct—the efforts of professional (to say nothing of amateur) reformers. Mr. Nader must flit from automobiles to drugs to local property assessments, cognizant that the public's interests and sympathies are not forever captureable by his vendetta against the Corvair. Recitals of ancient evil bore even a punctilious saint, so a constant supply of new charges against new villains must be uncovered or fabricated, and suitably printed in the hot ink of outrage. The self-appointed savior and his colleagues and legislative allies may get an occasional law. But they will not, year in and year out, attend the appropriation hearings, and the unending sequence of hearings on new appointments, which in the long run determine the direction and personnel of the regulatory agency.

The superiority of the traditional defenses of the individual—reliance upon his own efforts and the power of competition—lie precisely in the characteristics which distinguish them from public regulation. Each of the traditional defenses is available and working at all times—self-interest and competition are never passing fads. Each of the traditional defenses is available to individuals and small groups—changes in policy and adaptation to new circumstances do not require changes in the ponderous, expensive, insensitive machinery of a great state. It is of regulation that the consumer must beware.

A Sketch of the History of Truth in Teaching

The future is obscure, even to men of strong vision, and one would perhaps be wiser not to shoot arrows into it. For the arrows will surely hit targets that were never intended. Witness the arrow of consumerism.

It started simply enough: various people—and especially a young man named Nader—found automobiles less safe than they wished, and quite possibly than you would have wished. They demanded and in a measure obtained, if not safer cars, at least cars that were ostensibly safer. A considerable and expensive paraphernalia of devices became obligatory in new cars. These zealous patrons of the public furthermore insisted that defective products be corrected, and that damage arising in spite of the most conscientious efforts of the manufacturer should be his financial responsibility. Similar arrows were soon launched at at score of nonvehicular industries.

This quiver of truth and safety-minded arrows was thrown for a time at perfectly appropriate targets—business men accustomed to public abuse, who were naturally able to charge their customers for any amount of safety, frequent and successful lawsuits, and obloquy. But the arrows of reform pass through—if they hit at all—the targets at which they are aimed, and in 1973 they hit a professor. Evil day!

In that year a young man named Dascomb Henderson, a graduate of Harvard Business School (1969) and recently discharged as assistant treasurer of a respectable-sized corporation, sued his alma mater for imparting instruction since demonstrated to be false. This instruction—we may omit here its explicit and complex algebraic formulation—concerned the proper investment of working capital. One of Henderson's teachers at the Harvard school, a Professor Plessek, had thoroughly sold his students upon a sure-fire method of predicting short-term interest rate movements, based upon a predictive equation incorporating

Reprinted from *The Journal of Political Economy* (March/April 1973).

recent movements of the difference between high- and low-quality
bond prices, the stock of money (Plessek had a Chicago Ph.D.),
the number of "everything is under control" speeches given by
governors of the Federal Reserve Board in the previous quarter,
and the full-employment deficit. It was established in the trial
that the equation had worked tolerably well for the period
1960–68 (and Henderson was exposed to this evidence in Plessek's
course in the spring of 1969), but the data for 1969 and 1970, once
analyzed, made it abundantly clear that the equation was capable
of grostesquely erroneous predictions. Assistant Treasurer
Henderson, unaware of these later results, played the long-term
bond market with his corporation's cash, and in the process the
cash lost its surplus character. He was promptly discharged,
learned of the decline of the Plessek model, and sued.

This was a new area of litigation, and Henderson's attorney
deliberately pursued several lines of attack, in the hope that at
least one would find favor with the court:

1. Professor Plessek had not submitted his theory to sufficient
empirical tests: had he tried it for the decade of the 1950s, he
would have had less confidence in it.

2. Professor Plessek did not display proper scientific caution.
Henderson's class notes recorded the sentence: "I'll stake my
reputation as an econometrician that this model will not [engage
in intercourse with] a portfolio manager." This was corroborated
with a different verb by a classmate's notes.

3. Professor Plessek should have notified his former students
once the disastrous performance of his theory in 1969 and 1970
became known.

4. Harvard University was grossly negligent in retaining (and
hence certifying the professional competence of) an assistant
professor whose work had received humiliating professional
criticism (*Journal of Business* [April 1972]). Instead he had been
promoted to associate professor in 1972.

The damages asked were $500,000 for impairment of earning
power and $200,000 for humiliation.

Harvard and Professor Plessek asked for dismissal of the suit,
as frivolous and unfounded. Universities and teachers could not
be held responsible for honest errors, or all instruction would be
brought to a stop. Universities and professors could not be asked

to disseminate new knowledge to previous students—this would be intolerably costly. In the lower court these defenses prevailed, and Judge MacIntosh (Harvard, LL.B. 1938) asserted that university instruction and publication were preserved from such attacks by the First Amendment, the principle of academic freedom, an absence of precedent for such a complaint, and the established unreliability of academic lectures. On appeal, however, Judge Howlson (Yale, LL.B. 1940) remanded the case for trial on the merits, and in the course of reversing Judge MacIntosh's decision, remarked: "It seems paradoxical beyond endurance to rule that a manufacturer of shampoos may not endanger a student's scalp but a premier educational institution is free to stuff his skull with nonsense."

As the reader will know, Harvard and Professor Plessek won the case on the merits, but by a thin and foreboding margin. Only the facts that (1) the Plessek equation, as of 1969, looked about as good as most such equations, and (2) the plaintiff could not reasonably be expected to be informed of the failure of the equation as soon as two years after it was discovered—the lag in publication alone is this long—excused the errant professor. As for Harvard, it would have shared responsibility for the undisputed damage to the plaintiff if Plessek had been of slightly lower quality. So held the court of last resort, in a decision that professors read as carefully as a hostile book review.

The university world received the decision with what an elderly Englishman would call concern, and I would call pandemonium. Professional schools—medicine as well as business—were quick to realize its implications. Within a breathless three weeks, a professor in Cornell's medical school had sent an explicit retraction of his treatment of Parkinson's disease to the last ten year's graduates of the school. This proved to be only the first of a torrent of such actions, but well before that torrent had climaxed, at least ninety-five suits against universities and·teachers had been filed. Along with the "call-backs," as the retractions were called in honor of their automobile antecedents, the learned journals were flooded with statements of "errata" and confessions of error. A fair number of academic reputations fell suddenly and drastically.

The subsequent, explosively rapid expansion of litigation directed to error in teaching is not for this nonlegal writer to report. Many years and cases were required before a reasonably predictable set of rights and responsibilities could be estabished, and a man may find much to anger himself in these cases, whatever his position. That the lazy or stupid student was entitled to an exhaustive explanation for his failure in a course (*Anderson* v. *Regents*, 191 Cal. 426) was an intolerably expensive abberation—especially when the teacher was required to present a tape recording of the explanation. That a professor could not be held responsible for error in a field where truth and error frequently exchanged identities (*Neal* v. *Department of Sociology*, 419 Mich. 3), on the other hand, inevitably raised a challenge to the field to justify its existence. Rather than pursue either the main line of decisions or the aberrations, it seems preferable to look at the eventual effects of truth-in-teaching upon the universities. A conscientious observer must be cautious in his interpretation of the effect—even though the present essay is clearly exempt from challenge (*President Bowen* v. *Assistant Professor Holland* [329 N.J. 1121], a tenure case)—so the following remarks are best viewed as plausible hypotheses.

In general, the new responsibility rested heavily upon those most able to bear it: those fields in which classification of given material as true or excusably false versus inexcusably false was easiest to establish with near unanimity. Theological schools were virtually exempted, and, oddly enough, also computer science. Mathematics was exempted because one could always look up the answer, and political science because one couldn't. The branch of economics dealing with how to enrich a new nation ("economic development" was the title) was actually forbidden by the courts, on the ground that no university could pay for the damage its teachers did.

In those subjects where truth-in-teaching bore most heavily—those where incorrect knowledge was costly and demonstrable, as medicine, chemistry, and tax law—the classroom became a very different place. Students were *forbidden* by most universities to take notes, which were supplied by the teacher, and the sneaky device of a tape recorder with hidden microphone was combatted vigorously, if not always sucessfully. Harvard's defense proved to have content: teachers were unwilling to introduce new ideas, but it can be argued that the net balance was favorable: much ancient nonsense also vanished, and courses often were completed in two weeks.

The learned journals underwent a remarkable transformation. Let me quote the introductory paragraph of an article on the nature of short-run price fluctuations in commodity prices (*Review of Economics and Statistics* [August 1978]):

> The present essay presents a theory, with corroborating though inadequate evidence, that there is a set of nonrandom short-run movements in the price of "wheat." (The actual commodity analyzed is secret but will be revealed to professors on written waiver of responsibility.) The present essay is concerned only with methodology. Only the crudest beginning has been made, and it would be irresponsibly rash to venture money on the hypothesis. Also, the hypothesis is virtually identical with Reslet's (1967); I contribute chiefly a more powerful statistical technique (due to S. Stigler 1973), which has its own limitations. The regressions have been calculated three times, on different computers, with similar results.[1] The author will welcome, but not be surprised at, valid criticisms of the paper.

The superscript 1 referred to a footnote by the editor of the *Review*: "The Board of Overseers of Harvard Univeristy expresses concern at the measure of nonrandomness in the residuals, which, if the author were a Harvard professor, would require a full departmental review of the manuscript," No wonder one scholar complained that there was more warning against reading his article than against smoking marijuana cigarettes!

The longer-term effects of truth-in-teaching are another story, which I shall not seek even to summarize here. The historic step was the creation in 1981 of the Federal Bureau of Academic Reading, Writing, and Research (ARWR). This body soon established licenses for participation in scholarly activities, and the license became a prima facie defense against the charge of incompetence. No university which employed an unlicensed teacher could receive federal grants, which by 1985 averaged 99.7 percent of university revenue. A fortunate by-product of this reform was the exclusion of communists, classical liberals, foreigners, and men under 36 from the licensed fields of scholarship, and of statisticians from law schools. But, to repeat, this is another story.

Notes

CHAPTER TWO

1. For example

> Although competition can bear some admixture of regulation, it cannot be combined with planning to any extent we like without ceasing to operate as an effective guide to production. Nor is 'planning' a medicine which, taken in small doses, can produce the effects for which one might hope from its thoroughgoing application. Both competition and central direction become poor and inefficient tools if they are incomplete; they are alternative principles used to solve the same problem, and a mixture of the two means that neither will really work and that the result will be worse than if either system had been consistently relied upon. Or, to express it differently, planning and competition can be combined only by planning for competition but not by planning against competition.   (Friedrich A. Hayek, *The Road to Serfdom* [Chicago, 1944], p. 42)

And again,

> Yet agreement that planning is necessary, together with the inability of democratic assemblies to produce a plan, will evoke stronger and stronger demands that the government or some single individual should be given powers to act on their own responsibility. The belief is becoming more and more widespread that, if things are to get done, the responsible authorities must be freed from the fetters of democratic procedure. (p. 67)

Such passages are, however, warnings of the consequences of comprehensive socialization rather than arguments that it is inevitable.

2. For a recent restatement of this view by a person not identified with "conservative" views, see the essay by K. E. Boulding, "The Dimensions of Economic Freedom," in *The Nation's Economic Objectives*, ed. E. O. Edwards (Chicago, 1964), esp. pp. 119–20.

CHAPTER FOUR

1. See the essay by Viner, "Adam Smith and Laissez Faire," in *Adam Smith 1776–1926* (Chicago: University of Chicago Press, 1928).

2. McCulloch, a somewhat underrated man, again challenged Smith here; see "Navigation Laws," *Edinburgh Review*, May 1823.

3. Mill's essay elicited a brilliant attack by Macaulay, who turned Mill's argument that every man seeks only his own interests against the plea for universal suffrage: "That the property of the rich minority can be made subservient to the pleasures of the poor majority will scarcely be denied. But Mr. Mill proposes to give the poor majority power over the rich minority. Is it possible to doubt to what, on his own principles, such an argument must lead?" The argument is carried to an interesting prediction: "As for America, we appeal to the twentieth century" ("Mill's Essay on Government," in *Critical, Historical and Miscellaneous Essays* [New York, 1873] 2: 36–37, 40).

4. Royal Commission on Railways, *Evidence and Papers Relating to Railways in Ireland* (1866), pp. 126–30, 359–60.

5. He did make some reference to the incompetence of state action: "the great majority of things are worse done by the intervention of government, than the individuals most interested in the matter would do them, or cause them to be done, if left to themselves" (J. S. Mill, *Principles of Political Economy*, 1st ed. [London, 1848], bk. 2, p. 511). This argument does not play a major role in shaping his attitude, however.

6. Mill's famous essay, *On Liberty*, does little to reduce our uncertainty. It is here that he asserts: "Despotism is a legitimate mode of government in dealing with barbarians, provided the end be their improvement, and the means justified by actually effecting the ends. The laws which, in many countries on the Continent, forbid marriage unless the parties can show that they have the means of supporting a family, do not exceed the legitimate powers of the State.... As the principle of the individual liberty is not involved in the doctrine of Free Trade ... " (*The English Philosophers from Bacon to Mill* [Modern Library 1939], pp. 956, 1035, 1024). It is not easy to avoid the conclusion that for Mill "liberty" was conveniently well correlated with the forms of behavior of which he personally approved.

7. Thus McCulloch said of the post office: "It does not seem, though the contrary has been sometimes contended, that the Postoffice could be so well conducted by anyone else as by government: the latter alone can enforce perfect regularity in all its subordinate departments" (*Dictionary of Commerce* [1854 ed.], sv. "Postage").

8. It should be a source of morbid instruction to us, that immediately after laying down this dogmatic rule on how to treat with dangerous machinery, Jevons denounces those who view the economist as a "presumptuous theorist, who is continually laying down hard-and-fast rules for the conduct of other people" (*The State in Relation to Labour* [London, 1882], p. 8).

9. "Experimental Legislation and the Drink Traffic," *The Contemporary Review, 37* (1880): 192 (reprinted in *Methods of Social Reform*, p. 275). He did not see the potentialities of empirical study in the absence of formal experiment, however, and denied the feasibility of a statistical approach ("Experimental Legislation," pp. 184–85).

10. The maturing fruit in a later edition; *The Economics of Welfare*, 4th ed. (1932), p. 399.

CHAPTER FIVE

1. In our statistical work we measure regulation from three years after the creation of the commission, on impressionistic evidence of the lag involved in organizing the commission, hence all statements regarding, for example, states regulating in 1917 should be interpreted to refer to states initiating regulation no later than 1914.

2. The complete average rates are reported in Table A2 in the appendix [to this chapter.] These average revenues per kilowatt hour involve the following adjustments of census data: for 1907 to 1922 revenues include sales by private electric companies to ultimate consumers, domestic and industrial, plus net sales to out-of-state electric companies, municipal electric companies, and electric railroads, but exclude intercompany sales within states. KWH figures are for KWH's generated by private electric companies plus net purchases of KWH's from electric railroads or out-of-state electric companies. For 1927 to 1937 revenue and KWH data are for current sold to ultimate consumers, including gross sales to electric railroads but excluding all sales to other electric companies.

3. The finding that regulation may affect industrial and commercial rates is a possible clue to the reason public regulation was adopted [1974].

4. In 1924 the ratio of bills for 250 and 100 KWH is barely significant at the 5 percent level; the difference is opposite to that predicted as resulting from regulation.

5. The 1917 difference is significantly different from zero at the 5 percent level; the 1937 difference at the 10 percent level.

6. In 1937, 6 of 7 unregulated states had KWH per domestic buyer divided by KWH per industrial buyer above the mean of all states, but only 7 of 29 regulated states had ratios above the mean.

7. A separate termination in 1918 yields the same results.

8. An analysis of variance was also made of table 7, grouping states into four classes, by year of regulation: 1887, 1907–1910, 1911–1914, not regulated in 1920. No significant effect of regulation was found.

9. An elasticity of –8 implies that a utility will set prices 14 percent

above marginal cost. In the constant cost case, given a capital/sales ratio of 4, rates of return will exceed the competitive level by 3½ percent.

CHAPTER SIX

1. Eighty-eighth Cong., 1st Sess., House Document 95, 1963, *Report of the Special Study of the Securities Markets of the Securities and Exchange Commission* (Wash., D.C.: Government Printing Office, 1963), part 1. All citations in text to part, chapter, or page refer to this work.

2. The *Report* discusses only the higher rate of use of expulsion as a penalty against younger firms. The *Report* does not relate sanctions to violations so the interpretation of heavier penalties is obscure, even if the more lenient enforcement against older firms remarked upon by the *Report* is waived.

3. The section that follows was revised to incorporate the corrected data first presented in "Comment," *Journal of Business*, October 1964, pp. 414–22.

4. To choose a real and workable example, would an analysis of stock price relatives reveal any difference between issues of companies making annual financial reports and companies making quarterly financial reports? The desirability of the present registration requirement of a balance sheet not over three months old could then be determined.

5. An estimate of the role of dividends for two years in each period was made as follows: the aggregate dividends received on stocks issued in 1923 and 1924, and in 1950 and 1951, are expressed as rates of return on the initial costs to investors of the issues in the accompanying table. This sample suggests that dividends were a larger component of return in the 1920s.

RATE OF RETURN ON INITIAL COST

Year and Type of Issue	1924[a]	1925	1926	1927	1928
1923–24:					
Preferred........	7.11	7.10	6.77	6.50	6.30
Common..........	7.11	6.16	6.56	6.77	7.62

Year and Type of Issue	1951[b]	1952	1953	1954	1955
1950–51:					
Preferred........	6.89	4.78	4.81	4.86	4.81
Common..........	1.62	4.17	4.11	4.08	4.26

[a]1923 issues only.

[b]1950 issues only.

6. Of twenty-six issues of common stock in 1949–54, only six were by companies less than three years old; the corresponding figure for 1923–

27 was thirty-eight less than three years old of a total of fifty-three issues. Lawrence Fisher has suggested that the month-to-month fluctuations in the Standard and Poor Index were greater in the late 1920s and early 1930s than in recent years, so that the use of the annual average Standard and Poor Index in our deflations may account for a substantial portion of the greater variance obtained for the pre-SEC period.

7. The correlation coefficients for issue prices and prices one year later (in each case deflated by the Standard and Poor Index) were .76 in the 1920s (44 issues) and .96 in the 1950s (46 issues). The correlation coefficents for adjacent pairs of years after issue averaged .90 in the 1920s and .96 in the 1950s. The interpretation of these findings would be clearer if correlation coefficients were available for established issues and if the effects (if any) of size of issue were determined.

8. The costs of the program, that is, probably exceed even a reasonably optimistic estimate of benefits. Costs of flotations due to registration have apparently never been estimated even approximately; the SEC data (e.g., *Cost of Flotations*, 1945–49) exclude costs included in commissions of underwriters and costs of the delays imposed by the process, as well as costs of operating the SEC. The full costs of registration for new stock issues could be 5 percent of their value.

9. The *Special Study* shows particular concern with the specialist who "reaches across" the market, i.e., who initiates transactions by buying stock at the offer or selling at the bid, instead of waiting for someone to trade. This alarm again reflects the study's identification of the specialist's proper role with strict price stabilization. Suppose the bid is 30 and the ask 30½, and the specialist anticipates that the market will soon go to 32–32½. He buys at 30½ so the effective ask becomes (say) 30¾. He has initiated a price move, but one called for by his function of achieving equilibrium, if his anticipation is correct.

10. Of course, the frequency of transactions depends upon the size of the individual transactions, but this is not closely correlated with frequency. A short sequence of the transactions of the NYSE was tabulated for 5 November 1963 and is shown in the accompanying table.

No. of Transactions	No. of Stock Issues	Average Transaction Size(Shares)
1	264	225
2	97	181
3	51	199
4	30	190
5	13	192
6	12	303
7	3	200
8	3	196
9	3	144
12-16	9	172
18-67	3	236

11. This delay is the average of 7.59 units for the earlier tender plus zero units for the tender that makes a transaction. If we include bids or asks after twenty-five time units, the average delay is 8.04 units—perhaps a half-hour for an active stock, a week or a month for an inactive stock.

12. Specialists affect our model in the following ways: (1) the bid of 29¾ effectively eliminates all offers by non-dealers at less than 29¾, so the frequency distribution of offers now ranges from 29¾ to 31, with the lowest offer arising ½ of the time on average; (2) the offer of 30 effectively eliminates all bids by non-dealers at more than 30, with similar consequences.

13. In the absence of specialists, the gains or losses of buyers measured from an expected price of 29⅞ were exactly offset by the corresponding losses or gains for sellers. (We ignore commissions, which will be the same with or without specialists, at least as a first approximation.) The parties now lose the jobber's "turn" of (say) ¼, which is the price they pay for one of two things: (1) immediate availability of a buyer or seller; (2) the elimination of short run fluctuations in price. These two gains are analytically one: there is always an available buyer at a low enough price, and an available seller at a high enough price, so the gain of immediate marketability is at a price which contains no random elements. (Strictly speaking, we should say a price with much reduced random elements. The specialists' inventory will be exhausted from time to time when unusually long runs of bids or asks arise, since inventories will not be held in quantities sufficient to cope with the longest runs.)

With perfect foresight, the analysis would be modified in only one respect in order to be applied to changing equilibrium prices: the equilibrium price of a security could never fluctuate by more than the cost of holding it.

14. See Lester G. Telser, "A Theory of Speculation Relating Profitability and Stability," *Review of Economics and Statistics*, August 1959.

CHAPTER EIGHT

1. The domestic producers of petroleum, who also benefit from the import quota, would find a tariff or cash payment to domestic producers equally attractive. If their interests alone were consulted, import quotas would be auctioned off instead of being given away.

2. The Federal Home Loan Bank Board is the regulatory body. It also controls the amount of advertising and other areas of competition.

3. The largest refineries were restricted to 75.7 percent of their historical quota under the earlier voluntary import quota plan.

4. The ratio of trucks to total population would measure the product of (1) the importance of trucks to farmers, and (2) the importance of farmers in the state. For reasons given later, we prefer to emphasize (1).

5. This is known for each railroad, and we assume that (1) the average holds within each state, and (2) two or more railroads in a state may be combined on the basis of mileage. Obviously both assumptions are at best fair approximations.

6. If the deadweight loss (of consumer and producer surplus) is taken into account, even if the oil industry were in the majority it would not obtain the legislation if there were available some method of compensation (such as sale of votes) by which the larger damage of the minority could be expressed effectively against the lesser gains of the majority.

7. There is an organizational problem in any decision in which more than one vote is cast. If because of economies of scale it requires a thousand customers to buy a product before it can be produced, this thousand votes has to be assembled by some entrepreneur. Unlike the political scene, however, there is no need to obtain the consent of the remainder of the community, because they will bear no part of the cost.

8. The theory that the lobbying organization avoids the "free-rider" problem by selling useful services was proposed by Thomas G. Moore ("The Purpose of Licensing," *Journal of Law and Economics*, October 1961) and elaborated by Mancur Olson (*The Logic of Collective Action* [Cambridge, Mass.: Harvard University Press, 1965]). The theory has not been tested empirically.

9. Let n = the number of members of the profession and y = average income. We expect political capacity to be in proportion to (ny) so far as benefits go, but to reflect also the direct value of votes, so the capacity becomes proportional to $(n^a y)$ with $a > 1$.

10. We may pool the occupations and assign dummy variables for each occupation; the regression coefficients then are:

size of occupation relative to labor force: -0.450 ($t = 0.59$)
urbanization   : -12.133 ($t = 4.00$).

Thus urbanization is highly significant, while size of occupation is not significant.

11. A more precise analysis might take the form of a regression analysis such as:

Year of licensure = constant
               $+b_1$ (year of critical size of occupation)
               $+b_2$ (year of critical urbanization of occupation),

where the critical size and urbanization were defined as the mean size and mean urbanization in the year of licensure.

12. Lawyers, physicians, and pharmacists were all relatively large occupations by 1900, and nurses also by 1910. The only large occupation

to be licensed later was barbers; the only small occupation to be licensed early was embalmers.

13. The regulation of business in a partial market will also generally produce very high supply elasticities within a market: if the price of the product (or service) is raised, the pressure of excluded supply is very difficult to resist. Some occupations are forced to reciprocity in licensing, and the geographical dispersion of earnings in licensed occupations, one would predict, is not appreciably different than in unlicensed occupations with equal employer mobility. Many puzzles are posed by the interesting analysis of Arlene S. Holen in "Effects of Professional Licensing Arrangements on Interstate Labor Mobility and Resource Allocation," *Journal of Political Economy* 73 (1915): 492–98.

14. This position is presented more generally in "Political Competition and Economic Competition," *Public Choice*, Fall 1972.

15. Perhaps one should mention also an effect, if not purpose, of such studies: to contribute to the gradual realization that the self-interest theory holds in political life!

CHAPTER NINE

1. Using figure 1, let constant unit costs before regulation be OA, and after regulation OD. Demand will be larger for the safer product, but not enough larger to pay for the increment of safety, and output will fall—or the industry would have provided the safety voluntarily.

2. A qualification must be made if there are producer rents: then resources driven out of the industry by the regulation would pay something to be free of the regulation—and the resources may be owned by the entrepreneurs.

3. The long run is the life of existing entrepreneurs if they have special knowledge or skills in the regulated field.

4. If they do, and their demand curve is infinitely elastic, we have simply defined an activity improperly. We have, for example, imposed a tax on stock certificates whose serial number is prime, leaving all other numbers untaxed.

5. Less the costs of compliance and the consumer's share of the costs of enforcement.

6. In addition there are other social costs which might not be recorded directly in anyone's accounts. The delays, imposed by the regulatory process raised prices by more than 6 percent in one case; see Robert Gerwig, "Natural Gas Production: A Study of Costs of Regulation," *Journal of Law and Economics*, 1962.

7. The regression equation is $N = 12.86 + .0089\, E$ ($t = 2.62$) where N is number of cases and E is expenditure in thousands of 1945–47 dollars. This implies a marginal cost of $112,000.

8. See Richard A. Posner, "A Statistical Study of Antitrust Enforcement," *Journal of Law and Economics*, October 1970.

9. Expenditures are presumably the independent variable, certainly in the short run. If we regress expenditures on activities and take the reciprocal of that elasticity, we obtain the following estimates:

FHLB	.5
NLRB	1.2
Wage and Hour	1.0
ICC	–29.0
Antitrust	2.8

The fits of the equation of the last two agencies are much less close so the two regressions yield very different results.

10. It hardly seems worth calculating that the FCC spent $1 for each $550 of operating revenue of the industries it regulated in 1960, and that the corresponding figures were $1 per $1,000 for the ICC and $1 per $300 for the CAB, whereas the figure for the Antitrust Division would be rather more like $1 per $50,000.

11. The sources of the data are the annual reports of the Illinois Department of Finance and those of the individual agencies.

12. The basic tables are available upon request.

13. This budgetary characteristic is due at least partly to the fact that regulatory bodies are not explicitly charged for their housing.

14. The protective tariff which is administered by the customs service, has the characteristic of near-universality (as do the anti-trust agencies) and some element of irregularity of dealing with specific parties. It too has no fee system.

15. For the full variety of fees, see Federal Register, July 8, 1970.

16. Fees are sometimes based upon the rate of operation of the regulated parties. The SEC, for example, levies:

(1) 1/100 of 1 percent (= .0001) on the aggregate asking price of new issues (with a minimum of $100).

(2) 1/500 of 1 percent (= .00002) on the value of securities sold on security exchanges.

17. The industry would be better off because the quantity demanded of the industry's output would be larger and rents of specialized factors therefore larger.

18. This is an application of the argument in "Director's Law of Public Income Redistribution," *Journal of Law and Economics*, April 1970.

19. On occasion fees may also be used to achieve that most basic of all the industry's goals of public regulation, the control over entry. The costs of fees to enter could be set high relative to those of established firms.

20. The exception of agriculture is perhaps nominal: the state bodies are minuscule relative to the federal programs.

21. The author was a recent, improbable exception to this rule: he was a public member of the Board of Securities Investor Protection Corporation (SIPC), a nonprofit government-chartered corporation which insured security brokers, during 1971-73.

22. The numbers are not additive because some names are counted more than once, e.g., a man who had a subsequent political office and then entered law would appear twice.

23. A more recent study carries some of the Herring results to 1965; see D. T. Stanley, D. E. Mann, and J. W. Doig, *Men Who Govern* (The Brookings Institution, 1967). They find that 11 percent of the commissioners of the independent regulatory bodies were ex-congressmen (p. 141). Half of all commissioners were reappointed—a very large fraction when account is taken of age and changes in party (p. 154).

24. See "The Theory of Economic Regulation," *The Bell Journal of Economics and Management Science*, 1971 [chapter 8].

CHAPTER ELEVEN

1. *Government Price Statistics*, Hearings before the Subcommittee on Economic Statistics of the Joint Economic Committee, part 1, January 24, 1961, p. 35. Although I was chairman of this committee, I do not disqualify the quotation: there were seven other and distinguished members of that committee, and I would not wish to deny Manuel Cohen the right to quote bodies of which he has been chairman.

2. The case was Securities and Exchange Commission vs. Capital Gains Research Bureau, Inc. (84 Supreme Court Reporter 275, January 1, 1964). An exhibit of the seven instances of the practice complained against is given with the court's decision (84 Supreme Court Reporter 288), and a portion of it is reproduced in table 1 of this note. In addition, I have added two columns: (1) the price per share which would have been paid by investors buying immediately (within five days) after the recommendation to purchase the stock, (2) the price per share which would have been received by investors if they had sold within four days after the investment adviser sold the stock.

The main results are:

    (1) Investors would have lost slightly on two issues.

    (2) Investors would have gained slightly on four issues.

    (3) Investors would have gained substantially on the short sale.

    (4) Investors would have done as well, on average, as the adviser, in three stocks but less well in four stocks.

    (5) The average gain of investors would have been $1.33 per share, less commissions.

3. See chapter 6 of this volume. A sample result is reproduced in table 2.

TABLE 1

DATA PERTAINING TO CAPITAL GAINS
RESEARCH BUREAU CASE

	Average Price Per Share			
	5 days after purchase recommendation	4 days after Sale by Capital Gains Research Bureau	Purchase price of Capital Gains Research Bureau	Sale price of Capital Gains Research Bureau
Continental Insurance Co.	$49.94	$49.77	$47.78	$50.12
United Fruit Co.	24.73	23.48	21.69	24.06
Creole Petroleum Co.	27.69	28.75	27.00	28.06
Hart, Schaffner & Marx	25.11	25.31	23.00	25.06
Union Pacific	26.89	27.30	26.00	27.00
Frank G. Shattuck Co.	19.11	20.47	16.83	19.81
Chock Full o'Nuts (short sale)	69.18	62.34	68.88	62.25

TABLE 2

AVERAGE PRICES OF SELECTED NEW ISSUES RELATIVE TO
COMPREHENSIVE STANDARD AND POOR INDEX
(Issue Year = 100)

Period	Year After Issue				
	1	2	3	4	5
1923-27	89.9	77.9	72.5	66.2	70.7
1949-55	87.9	79.1	78.4	77.7	74.9

4. For a remarkable study of the review of new drugs, which on balance assigns heavy costs to the program, see S. Peltzman, "An Evaluation of Consumer Protection Legislation: The 1962 Drug Amendments," *Journal of Political Economy* 81 (1973): 1049–91.

5. See R. Kessel, "Economic Effects of Federal Regulation of Milk Markets," *Journal of Law and Economics*, October 1964.

6. Robert Fellmeth, *The Interstate Commerce Commission* (Grossman Publishers, Inc., 1970).

Index

Index